INTRODUCTION

# THEORETICAL UNDERPINNINGS

## Psychotherapy Integration

Psychotherapy integration is characterized by dissatisfaction with single-school approaches and a concomitant desire to look across school boundaries to see how patients can benefit from other ways of conducting psychotherapy (Norcross & Goldfried, 2005). We attempt to tailor psychological treatments and therapeutic relationships to the specific and varied needs of individual patients as defined by a multitude of diagnostic and particularly transdiagnostic considerations. We do so by systematically drawing on effective methods across theoretical schools (integrative) and by matching those methods to particular clients on the basis of evidence-based principles.

Psychotherapy universally applied as one-size-fits-all is proving impossible and, in some cases, even unethical. Of course, giving every patient the same brand of psychotherapy would simplify treatment selection, but it flies in the face of what we know about individual differences, patient preferences, and disparate cultures.

The clinical reality is that no single psychotherapy proves effective for all patients and situations, no matter how good it is for some. That is the driving force behind integration, the modal theoretical orientation of psychotherapists in Western developed countries. Evidence-based practice has come to demand flexible and individualized, if not integrative, treatment.

Imposing a parallel situation onto other health care professions drives the point home. To take a medical metaphor, would you entrust your health to a physician who prescribed the identical treatment (say, antibiotics or neurosurgery) for every patient and illness encountered? Or, to take an educational analogy, would you prize instructors who employed the same pedagogical method (say, a lecture) for every educational opportunity? Or would you entrust your child to a child-care worker who delivers the identical response (say, a nondirective attitude or a slap on the bottom) to every child and every misbehavior? "No" is probably your resounding answer. Psychotherapy clients deserve no less consideration.

On the face of it, of course, virtually every clinician endorses fitting the therapy to the individual client. After all, who can seriously dispute the notion that psychological treatment should be tailored to the specific needs of the patient? Indeed, treatment manuals are increasingly focusing on ways to be flexible—but they still work within a confined set of theoretical parameters and technical procedures. In contrast, integrative therapy goes beyond this simple acknowledgment of the need for flexibility in several ways:

- Our integrative therapy is derived directly from outcome research rather than from an idiosyncratic theory or seat-of-the-pants syncretism.
- Our therapy embraces the potential contributions of multiple systems of psychotherapy rather than working from within a single theoretical system.
- Our treatment selection is predicated on diagnostic and several transdiagnostic client characteristics, in contrast to relying on patient diagnosis alone.
- Our aim is to offer optimal treatment methods and healing relationships, whereas many focus narrowly on selecting methods. Both interventions and relationships, both the instrumental and the interpersonal—intertwined as they are—are required in effective psychotherapy.
- Our integrative therapy occurs throughout the course of treatment (not only at pretreatment as case formulation), tracks client progress, and evolves with the client through termination. Clients evolve and progress—and their initial complaints are not necessarily their primary disorders or goals at the conclusion of treatment.

In the past, we as well as our colleagues have invoked a plethora of terms to describe our aim to fit the treatment to the patient: prescriptive eclectic, systematic treatment selection, differential therapeutics, responsiveness, aptitude by treatment interaction, customizing, and so on. Here, we employ the term *integrative* throughout. We do so in recognition of (a) the term's more inclusive connotation and representation of psychotherapy integration, (b) its broader acceptance and use in clinical circles than the alternative terms, and (c) its emerging preference among mental

health professionals as their self-identification (Norcross, Karpiak, & Lister, 2005).

In the past, too, integrative supervision was driven by the notion of "different strokes for different folks," but the philosophical pluralism was not concretely translated into sophisticated matching. Typically, that matching was based on a single, static patient characteristic—the presenting problem or diagnosis. Today, by contrast, the matching or fit is driven by multiple client features, especially transdiagnostic characteristics, such as stage of change, reactance level, patient preferences, and culture.

## Integrative Supervision

These cardinal principles of integrative therapy similarly apply to integrative supervision and working with trainees. No single supervision theory or method is effective for all supervisees and situations, no matter how good it is for some. Evidence-based supervision has come to demand a flexible, if not integrative, perspective.

There are numerous pathways to the integration of the psychotherapies and thus multiple approaches to integrative supervision. The four predominant pathways are common factors, technical eclecticism, theoretical integration, and assimilative integration. All four are characterized by a desire to look beyond the confines of single theories and the techniques traditionally associated with them, but they do so in rather different ways and at different levels. Below we summarize these four routes to integration and comment on their implications for the supervision enterprise.

### *Common Factors*

The common factors approach seeks to determine the core ingredients that different therapies share, with the eventual goal of creating more parsimonious and efficacious treatments based on those commonalities. This search is predicated on the belief that commonalities are more important in accounting for therapy outcome than are the unique factors that differentiate among them. The research-informed models of Jerome Frank (1973) and Bruce Wampold (Wampold & Imel, 2015) exemplify the

common factors route. Marvin Goldfried (1980, p. 996), a leader of the integration movement, argued,

> [to] the extent that clinicians of varying orientations are able to arrive at a common set of strategies, it is likely that what emerges will consist of robust phenomena, as they have managed to survive the distortions imposed by the therapists' varying theoretical biases.

In specifying what is common across orientations, we may also be selecting what works best among them.

Judging from experience and the literature (Castonguay, 2000), some psychotherapy supervision is conducted from an explicit common factors perspective. Supervisors enjoin their trainees to cultivate therapeutic commonalities, such as development of a therapeutic alliance, opportunity for validation, acquisition and practice of new behaviors, and fostering positive expectancies (Grencavage & Norcross, 1990; Weinberger, 1995), in their therapy sessions just as supervisors symmetrically do so in supervision sessions. When these common factors operate in "good enough" fashion, they converge to produce favorable supervision outcomes, such as reducing trainee shame and self-doubt, enhancing identity development, and increasing competence development (Watkins, Budge, & Callahan, 2015).

The dilemma is that one cannot function "commonly" or "nonspecifically" in therapy or training (Omer & London, 1988). Hence we must operationalize specific clinical behaviors associated with common factors for purposes of supervision. Until such time, integrative supervision from a common factors perspective will be largely relegated to the prevalent, but still frequently unheeded, reminder that the so-called common factors in psychotherapy—principally the therapeutic relationship—account for more outcome variance than do technical interventions (Norcross & Lambert, 2014).

More than commonalities are evident across the therapies; unique or specific factors are attributable to different therapies as well. One of the seminal achievements of psychotherapy research is demonstration of the differential effectiveness of psychotherapies with a few disorders and with specific types of people. Integrative supervision thus emphasizes those factors

common across therapies while capitalizing on the contributions of specific techniques. The proper use of common *and* specific factors will probably be most effective for clients and most congenial to supervisors (Garfield, 1992; Watkins et al., 2015); that is, we will gradually integrate by combining fundamental similarities and useful differences across the schools.

## *Technical Eclecticism*

Eclectics seek to improve the ability to select the best treatments for the person and the problem on the basis of clinical experience and empirical research. The focus is on predicting for whom interventions will work; the foundation is actuarial rather than theoretical (Lazarus, Beutler, & Norcross, 1992). Proponents of technical eclecticism use procedures drawn from different sources without necessarily subscribing to the theories from which they originated. For technical eclectics, no necessary connection exists between metabeliefs and techniques. As Lazarus (1967, p. 416) described it, "To attempt a theoretical rapprochement is as futile as trying to picture the edge of the universe. But to read through the vast amount of literature on psychotherapy, in search of techniques, can be clinically enriching and therapeutically rewarding."

In practice and in supervision, this integrative approach is widely exemplified in Arnold Lazarus's multimodal therapy and Larry Beutler's (Beutler & Clarkin, 1990) systematic treatment selection. Our approach to psychotherapy supervision and much of this book emanate from the eclectic mandate to customize the technical interventions and the relationship stance to the unique needs of each individual. This customizing or matching, it should be emphasized, applies with equal cogency to trainees assisting their clients and to supervisors assisting their trainees. Integrative supervisors are continually involved in a parallel process of tailoring their supervision to the individual student and enhancing their student's ability to tailor psychological treatment to individual clients.

## *Theoretical Integration*

In this pathway to psychotherapy integration, two or more therapies are synthesized in the hope that the result will be better than the constituent

therapies alone. Theoretical integration aspires to more than a simple combination; it seeks an emergent theory that is more than the sum of its parts, and that leads to new directions for practice and research. As the name implies, there is an emphasis on integrating the underlying theories of psychotherapy—what London (1966) eloquently labeled "theory smushing"—along with the integration of therapy techniques from each—what London has called "technique melding." Theoretical integration represents the most popular variant of integration among clinical and counseling psychologists in the United States (Lichtenberg, Goodyear, Overland, Hutman, & Norcross, 2016).

Paul Wachtel's (1977, 1987) influential efforts to bridge psychoanalytic, behavioral, and interpersonal theories illustrate this direction, as do efforts to blend cognitive and psychoanalytic therapies, notably Anthony Ryle's (1990) cognitive–analytic therapy. Grander schemes have been advanced to meld most of the major systems of psychotherapy, such as the transtheoretical approach (involving the stages of change) of James Prochaska and Carlo DiClemente (1984; Prochaska & Norcross, 2013). All of these stop short, however, of a grand unifying theory of psychotherapy (Magnavita & Anchin, 2014), which may or may not eventually prove possible.

Psychotherapists combine multiple theories in creating their integrations. When 187 self-identified integrative psychologists rated their use of six major theories (behavioral, cognitive, humanistic, interpersonal, psychoanalytic, systems), the resulting 15 dyads were each selected by at least one therapist (Norcross et al., 2005). The most common dyad endorsed in the mid 1970s was psychoanalytic–behavioral (Garfield & Kurtz, 1977); in the mid 1980s, the three most popular hybrids all involved cognitive therapy (Norcross & Prochaska, 1988); and in the early 2000s, cognitive therapy dominated the list of combinations. Cognitive therapy also accounted for 42% of the hybrid combinations in the United States, less so in other countries.

Supervisors combining two theoretical models, say, cognitive–behavioral therapy (CBT) and mindfulness/acceptance therapy, would certainly be recognized as theoretical integrationists. But as soon as another

theoretical model is invoked in supervision, integration seems to merge into eclecticism; that is, in supervision, the distinctions among technical eclecticism and theoretical integration are rarely apparent or functional. Few supervisees receiving broadband supervision could distinguish between them. Moreover, we hasten to add that these integrative strategies are not mutually exclusive. No technical eclectic can totally disregard theory, and no theoretical integrationist can ignore technique.

## *Assimilative Integration*

The fourth route to integration entails a firm grounding in one system of psychotherapy, with a willingness to selectively incorporate (assimilate) practices and views from other systems (Messer, 1992). In doing so, assimilative integration combines the advantages of a single, coherent theoretical system with the flexibility of a broader range of techniques from multiple systems. A cognitive therapist, for example, might use the gestalt two-chair dialogue in an otherwise behavioral course of treatment. In addition to Stanley Messer's (1992, 2001) original explication of it, exemplars of assimilative integration are George Stricker and Jerold Gold's (1996) assimilative psychodynamic therapy and Louis Castonguay and associates' (2004) cognitive–behavioral assimilative therapy.

To its proponents, assimilative integration is a realistic way station to a sophisticated integration; to its detractors, it is more of a waste station of people unwilling to commit to an evidence-based integration. Both sides agree that assimilation is a partial step toward full integration; most therapists have been and continue to be trained in a single approach, and most gradually incorporate parts and methods of other approaches once they discover the limitations of their original approach.

The personal journeys of seasoned psychotherapists (e.g., Dryden & Spurling, 1989; Goldfried, 2001) suggest that this is how therapists actually modify their clinical practices and expand their repertoires. Therapists do not discard original ideas and practices but rework them, add to them, and cast them in new forms. They gradually, inevitably assimilate new methods into their home theory (and life experiences) to formulate an effective treatment.

In assimilative supervision, then, trainees would be taught primarily from a single theoretical tradition with the occasional use of a method aligned with another theoretical system. How often and on what basis supervisees depart from their primary theory remains to be ascertained, but such departure is certainly a frequent and realistic step toward more ambitious integrative supervision.

In our integrative supervision, we heartily embrace three of these routes to integration: common factors, especially for its focus on the therapeutic and supervisory relationship and its emphasis on principles/processes of change; technical eclecticism, which tailors or fits psychotherapy to the unique needs of each client and correspondingly supervision to the individuality of each trainee based on empirical research; and theoretical integration, which demonstrates that theoretical systems are often complementary, not contradictory, when embedded within the diversity of treatment goals, patient preferences, stages of change, and other transdiagnostic features. We do not highlight assimilative integration further in this book as it represents only a cautious half-step toward a full integrative supervision.

## HISTORICAL PERSPECTIVE

A novice psychotherapist is faced with a proverbial tower of Babel. He or she is immediately confronted with an overwhelming diversity of theoretical orientations, each represented by articulate and adamant advocates and equally articulate and adamant detractors. The confusion of ideas and admonitions, do's and don'ts, is likely to dampen the enthusiasm of all but the most resilient of students. Integrative approaches to psychotherapy supervision, like integrative psychotherapies themselves, offer hope of reconciliation among diverse orientations and provide an anchor of empiricism in a sea of theory.

Integration as a point of view has probably existed as long as philosophy and psychotherapy. In philosophy, the 3rd-century biographer Diogenes Laertius referred to an eclectic school that flourished in Alexandria in the 2nd century (Lunde, 1974). In psychotherapy, Freud

consciously struggled with the selection and integration of diverse methods. As early as 1919, he introduced psychoanalytic psychotherapy as an alternative to classical psychoanalysis in recognition that the more rarified approach lacked universal applicability (Liff, 1992).

More formal ideas on synthesizing the psychotherapies appeared in the literature as early as the 1930s (Goldfried, Pachankis, & Bell, 2005). For example, Thomas French (1933) stood before the 1932 meeting of the American Psychiatric Association and drew parallels between certain concepts of Freud and of Pavlov. In 1936, Saul Rosenzweig published an article that highlighted commonalities among various systems of psychotherapy (Rosenzweig, 1936). These and other early attempts at integration, however, were largely theory driven and empirically untested.

If not conspiratorially ignored altogether, these precursors to integration appeared only as a latent theme in a field organized around discrete theoretical orientations. Although psychotherapists secretly recognized that their orientations did not adequately assist them in all they encountered in practice, a host of political, social, and economic forces—such as professional organizations, training institutes, and referral networks—kept them penned within their own theoretical school yards and typically led them to avoid clinical contributions from alternative orientations.

Integrative supervision was probably inaugurated in the modern era by Frederick Thorne (1957, 1967) and Arnold Lazarus (1967), who are credited as the grandfathers of eclecticism. Persuasively arguing that any skilled professional should come prepared with more than one tool, Thorne emphasized the need for clinicians to fill their toolboxes with methods drawn from many different theoretical orientations. He likened contemporary psychotherapy to a plumber who used only a screwdriver. Like such a plumber, inveterate therapists applied the same treatment to all people, regardless of individual differences, and expected the patient to adapt to the therapist rather than vice versa. Lazarus's influential multimodal therapy inspired a generation of mental health professionals to think and behave more broadly.

In the late 1970s, several attempts at theoretical integration were introduced. Wachtel authored the classic *Psychoanalysis and Behavior*

*Therapy: Toward an Integration*, which attempted to bridge the chasm between the two systems. His integrative book began, ironically, in an effort to write an article portraying behavior therapy as "foolish, superficial, and possibly even immoral" (Wachtel, 1977, p. xv). But in preparing his article, he was forced for the first time to look closely at what behavior therapy was and to think carefully about the issues. When he observed some of the leading behavior therapists of the day, he was astonished to discover that the particular version of psychodynamic therapy toward which he had been gravitating dovetailed considerably with what a number of behavior therapists were doing. Wachtel's experience serves as a sage reminder that isolated theoretical schools perpetuate caricatures of other schools, thereby foreclosing changes in viewpoint and preventing expansion in practice.

The transtheoretical (across theories) approach of Prochaska and DiClemente was also introduced in the late 1970s with the publication of one of the first integrative textbooks, *Systems of Psychotherapy: A Transtheoretical Analysis* (Prochaska, 1979). This book reviewed different theoretical orientations from the standpoint of common change principles and of the stages of change. The transtheoretical approach in general, and the stages of change in particular, are among the most extensively researched integrative therapies (Schottenbauer, Glass, & Arnkoff, 2005).

Only within the past 40 years, then, has psychotherapy integration developed into a clearly delineated area of interest. The temporal course of interest in psychotherapy integration, as indexed by both the number of publications and the development of organizations and journals (Goldfried et al., 2005), reveals occasional stirrings before 1970, a growing interest during the 1970s, and rapidly accelerating interest from 1980 to the present. To put it differently, integrative psychotherapy has a long past but a short history as a systematic movement. Within that movement, publications on integrative training and supervision began appearing regularly in the 1980s (e.g., Beutler et al., 1987; Norcross, 1988; Norcross et al., 1986). In that sense, explicit integration is a relative newcomer to clinical supervision.

Integration itself represents only the first step: We therapists must widen our therapeutic repertoire and embrace multiple therapeutic

techniques, relationships, and formats. The second and empirical step is to specifically know when and where to use these multiple techniques, relationships, and formats. The early integrative supervisors favored a pragmatic blending (e.g., Halgin, 1985) but did not have the research evidence to specify when and how those multiple theories were to be blended. That robust evidence became available only in the past 2 decades (e.g., Beutler & Harwood, 2000; Norcross, 2011), leading to the systematic and research-informed brand of integrative supervision offered in this book.

## DEFINITION OF *SUPERVISION*

Clinical supervision essentially involves a human relationship with the intent of modifying the behaviors, affects, and cognitions of supervisees in ways that enable them to provide more effective (or efficient) services to their patients (Hess, 1980). It is, first and foremost, a relationship. Our insistence on defining supervision as a relationship leads us to eschew characterizations that define it primarily as a "professional practice" or "competence" (APA, 2015). Supervision is assuredly both of those, but the essential foundation, the sine qua non, is the relationship.

The parameters of supervision are fluid and permeable. Supervision extends over a circumscribed period in most instances but extends over decades in others. Supervision requires a distinct set of skills and knowledge, beyond those associated with being a competent practitioner, but clinical skills overlap considerably with supervision skills. Its purposes are multiple and occasionally conflicting: to mentor, to teach, to serve clients being treated by the supervisee and, of course, to evaluate and perhaps to gatekeep by weeding out unqualified professionals (Bernard & Goodyear, 2014).

### Teach Versus Treat

Supervision and psychotherapy share numerous features. They both comprise privileged, intimate relationships in which the supervisor/therapist assists supervisees/clients in examining their thoughts, feelings, and behaviors. The typical behaviors of the supervisor and therapist align: listening,

reflecting, empathizing, observing, providing information, offering feedback, and occasionally instructing. Both supervisees and clients are asked to share sensitive, often painful material in regularly scheduled sessions. Supervisees and clients alike desire awareness, skills, and anxiety relief, seeking change and resisting it at the same time. Both seek affirmation and fear judgment from the more powerful supervisor/therapist.

These marked structural similarities raise the legendary temptation to blend teaching and treating, to turn supervision into psychotherapy. Such circumstances rapidly become ethical, legal, and training landmines. For example, when discussing their countertransference to a particular client, supervisees may divulge too much personal information regarding the origin of their positive or negative feelings about their clients. Or supervisors may subtly pull or overtly demand such detailed information.

Supervisors can remain vigilant and remember that, although supervisees have the opportunity and right to seek therapy, they rarely have a choice regarding whether to seek supervision. Supervision and the particular supervisor are frequently mandated. Supervisors may slip into their preferred mode of conducting therapy, or supervisees may attempt to use supervision (knowingly or unknowingly) as their personal therapy. Supervisors need to mentor and maintain appropriate boundaries for their supervisees.

Despite the structural similarities of supervision and therapy, their goals differ substantively. The goals of supervision are to help the trainee develop his or her skills, model boundaries, offer support, and ensure client welfare. Clients seek treatment to enhance life satisfaction and work on specific behavioral disorders (Page & Wosket, 2001); in contrast, supervisees work toward an academic degree and often seek to become more advanced clinicians. This supervisory relationship is not a place to offer personal therapy to the supervisee (Watkins, 1997).

Some models of supervision suggest blurring the boundaries between supervision and therapy as long as it enables the supervisee to learn from the experience and become a more advanced clinician (Sarnat, 1992, 2015). We do not blur those boundaries. In integrative supervision, we conscientiously do not cross the boundaries between supervision and therapy.

Although one hopes that supervisees are mentally healthy and fit for their profession, there are times when their personal problems interfere with their ability to treat clients properly. When such difficulties arise, we as supervisors acknowledge what has occurred, discuss it openly with the supervisee, arrive at a mini remediation plan to avoid a reoccurrence, make a mental note to watch for it again, and then move on from the specific incident. Should the single incident prove a regular occurrence or constitute a serious breach, then integrative supervisors strongly recommend personal therapy. A referral for therapy can gently nudge supervisees into an appropriate therapeutic environment. When we recognize that supervisees' recurrent problems prevent them from providing good therapy, we do not attempt to treat the supervisee directly.

## Evidence-Based Practice and Competencies

The international juggernaut of evidence-based practice (EBP) lends increased urgency to the task of using the best available research and clinician expertise to tailor psychological treatment to the client's culture, personality, and goal (Norcross, Beutler, & Levant, 2006). In corresponding fashion, evidence-based supervision will leverage the best available research and supervisor expertise to tailor supervision to the unique trainee. Data-based clinical decision making will become the norm for conducting psychotherapy and for conducting supervision.

EBP has sped the breakdown of traditional schools and the escalation of informed pluralism (Norcross, Hogan, Koocher, & Maggio, 2017). EBP reflects a pragmatic commitment to "what works for whom." The clear emphasis is on what works, not on what theory the supervisor prefers. Integrative supervision is simpatico with EBP properly defined.

At the same time, our integrative supervision reflects and reinforces the growing movement toward competency education in mental health. The APA (2015) guidelines, for a recent exemplar, are organized under seven competency domains: supervisor competence; diversity; relationships; professionalism; assessment/evaluation/feedback; problems of professional competence; and ethical, legal, and regulatory considerations.

Although supervisor competence is often assumed, only recently has there been a shift by training programs to value competency-based supervision (Kaslow, Falender, & Grus, 2012). At the least, supervisors are expected to have informed and contemporary knowledge of research on supervision and the professional activities being supervised. Supervisors are expected to complete continued education in supervision via seminars and/or reaching out to another supervisor for their own supervision. In addition, supervisors should prioritize communication with other professionals responsible for the supervisee's continued learning and growth process and enable a direct line of contact between all supervisors.

However, competencies are not for the supervisor alone. Competency benchmarks can be usefully incorporated into the trainee's learning goals and into the criteria for the supervisor's evaluation of the trainee's performance. As detailed in later chapters, we adopt APA's competency benchmarks for different levels of training (Fouad et al., 2009) in completing written evaluations of the supervisee. For now, the take-home point is that our integrative supervision values and employs competencies for all parties involved.

## AUTHORS' PATHS

### John C. Norcross (Supervisor)

For 30-plus years, I have been supervising students and colleagues. My earliest flirtations with clinical supervision involved brief episodes of supervising less experienced doctoral students in a "vertical team" during my graduate studies. My primary lessons from that experience? First, I enjoyed the relational and clinical immediacy of supervision, and second, I learned to never arrange for two supervisors holding discordant theoretical orientations to supervise the same beginning student. Confusion reigns, and clients probably suffer.

In receiving graduate and postgraduate supervision, I was fortunate in many respects. I did not experience any awful or traumatizing supervisors. One supervisor was warm, supportive, but probably otherwise benign (teaching me the valuable lesson that quality supervision may

require a strong supervisory relationship, but more than that). Another clinical supervisor was wise, scholarly, but preferred to speak only of my research (teaching me that not all licensed professionals are interested or skilled in psychotherapy supervision). Otherwise, I obtained excellent and responsive supervision. In addition, I emerged as one of the lucky ones in that I completed a graduate course in supervision (actually, consultation and supervision), joining the 20% of psychologists serving as supervisors who received formal training in supervision (Peake, Nussbaum, & Tindell, 2002).

As well, I had the good fortune to be integratively trained by my family of origin and in my formal education, which obviated the need to take a circuitous and necessarily assimilative approach (Norcross, 2006). In some ways, my integrative perspective was overdetermined by my family of origin. I am the second of four children, all boys. Consistent with that ordinal position and the cumulative research (Sulloway, 1996), I was born to both mediate and rebel—an apt summary of integration. Reliable adult observers concur that I served as the go-between for my brothers and as the bridge between my older, domineering brother and my two younger siblings—a familiar pattern (or reconstruction) among psychotherapists in general (Dryden & Spurling, 1989; Henry et al., 1971). More than that, my birth order and family dynamics led to an openness to scientific innovation, along with a propensity to rebel against conventional wisdom.

Additionally and concurrently, I was a product of the synthesis of diverse religions and cultures. My parents hailed from different parts of the country: one from the urban northeast and another from the rural Smoky Mountains. Gentile and Jew, white collar and blue collar alike, populated our neighborhood and friendships. It was natural and easy to accommodate several religions in my extended family; for example, I attended a Jewish nursery school and kindergarten, a private Lutheran elementary school, a public high school, an originally Dutch Reform college, and a state university for graduate studies. (Continuing the theme, I married a woman raised as a Baptist, we attend a Methodist church, my stepdaughter and son attended private Catholic schools, and for the past 30 years, I have taught at a Jesuit university.)

These multiple traditions flowed naturally, like a seamless mosaic. A favorite family story is illustrative: When a young boy, I was asked if I was Jewish. Reflecting my multireligious heritage (or confusion), I replied, "No, but I think my brother is."

The occupational and political positions of my parents also profoundly influenced my worldview. My father was a labor organizer in his early years, when it was a radical—and potentially dangerous—profession, especially in the south where he met my mother. It was made clear to me that orthodoxy, dogma, and business were not to be trusted. My mother was one of the first female employees of the National Park Service, an adventuresome and unconventional position in the 1950s. Mistrust of the establishment and advocacy for the common people were leitmotifs.

In retrospect, my family shaped my personality in three directions that Robertson (1979) identified as facilitating integration among psychotherapists. First is an obsessive–compulsive drive to pull together all of the interventions of the therapeutic universe. Second is a maverick or rebellious temperament to move beyond theoretical monism. And third is a skeptical attitude toward the status quo. To these I would add being predisposed toward pragmatic considerations as opposed to theoretical doctrines—a variable also supported by the nascent research on integrative therapists.

Integrative leanings evident in childhood were crystallized by multiple undergraduate experiences. Undergraduate mentors modeled and demonstrated the integrative spirit. My three Rutgers mentors hailed from different orientations: Andrew Bondy was a staunch behaviorist; Michael Wogan was an interpersonal psychodynamicist (and a student of Hans Strupp); and Winnie Lennoix was a client-centered and multicultural therapist. Although strongly prizing their own orientations, they were uniformly respectful of the contributions of disparate traditions. All repeatedly emphasized that I would learn from complementary ways of researching and conducting psychotherapy. And, in applying to graduate school, Rutgers's Arnie Lazarus—one of the grandparents of eclecticism—guided my path.

The PhD program in clinical psychology at the University of Rhode Island (URI) cemented the integrative "deal." Jim Prochaska, with a recently relocated Carlo DiClemente in Texas, had just secured his first

multi-million-dollar grant for self-change and was building an impressive research program at URI. He had published *Systems of Psychotherapy: A Transtheoretical Analysis*, one of the first integrative texts on psychotherapy, taught couples therapy, and maintained a private practice. Here was a scientist–practitioner in action.

The URI clinical program provided unsystematic training in multiple theoretical traditions, but Jim's transtheoretical model brought it to a harmonious whole. The systematic synthesis of theoretical orientations was guided by the stages of change model, which was emerging in the research and then applied to clinical practice. The integration of research and practice was never explicitly presented as the scientist–practitioner or Boulder model—it simply occurred. Individual psychotherapy in the clinic was naturally blended with population-based interventions in the lab. Self-change was integrated with formal psychotherapy. These proved not contradictory but complementary.

Jim also supported my research expansion into the person of the therapist. We conducted several studies on the personal and professional characteristics of clinical psychologists and continue to chronicle the evolution of the field every few years. This work frequently highlighted that integration or eclecticism was the modal orientation of mental health professionals in the United States. Some of our most exciting projects examined the self-change experiences of psychotherapists. We discovered that psychotherapists' theories exert considerable influence on their treatment of clients but virtually none on the treatment of themselves (Prochaska & Norcross, 1983). This pattern of results has now been replicated in five studies with different populations and diverse disorders (Norcross & Aboyoun, 1994) and supports the notion that psychotherapists are quite secular, pragmatic, and integrative in their own self-change.

Regarding integration per se, a formal course on the topic was not offered in the URI clinical psychology program (until years after graduation, when I returned to teach it during a summer session). Nor did we employ the self-characterization of *integrative* until years later. More important, however, was the research-informed pluralism and the absence of the demeaning rivalry of paradigms.

Like most psychotherapists (Geller, Norcross, & Orlinsky, 2005), my personal therapy was personally rewarding and professionally instrumental. During graduate training, I undertook individual therapy with a psychodynamic therapist who was integrative and practical. I experienced little conflict in his being a psychoanalytic therapist or his being a psychiatrist. Instead, I warmly recall his interpersonal generosity—reducing session fees, seeing me at an earlier time—and his gentle directness. Toward the end of therapy, he supported my decision to decline attractive employment offers from doctorate-granting, research-intensive institutions. The fit would have been disastrous in the long run: They were principally interested in my writing articles, securing grants, and continually publishing but would have largely neglected my abiding interests in teaching, supervision, and practice. My therapist helped me see and secure what I wanted: a midsized institution that would allow me to teach, supervise, research multiple areas, edit, and practice minus the preoccupation with grant procurement.

My path toward becoming an integrative supervisor surely was nurtured in graduate training but rooted in my family of origin and undergraduate years. One's professional motives are less academic and more personal in origin than one may wish to consciously concede (Demorest, 2004). The personal is the professional, and this role fusion—the personal as the professional—runs throughout my career and my life.

Now, 30-plus years postdoctorate, I supervise 4.5 hours per week: 1.5 hours of group supervision with advanced undergraduates undertaking their first clinical fieldwork and 3 hours of individual supervision with postdoctoral psychologists and other mental health professionals interested in integrative psychotherapy. The latter, I immediately concede, is a privileged position; I determine how much to supervise and select whom I will supervise. That's my strong recommendation to other supervisors, but one not realistically available to most who labor in the vineyard.

## Leah M. Popple (Supervisee)

Although my path to integration is still in its infancy, and albeit a shorter version than that of JCN, it begins with my family of origin. I am the

second born, first daughter, in a family of four preceded by a brother and followed by my sister and then younger brother. I was born to working-class parents and the first in my family to complete a bachelor's degree. I attended Catholic grade school, public high school, and a large state university. This was followed by a Catholic graduate school and then internship, postdoc, and a position at a Jesuit university.

My undergraduate training at Pennsylvania State University offered me endless research opportunities in which I gladly indulged. I served as a research assistant in developmental psychology, clinical psychology, sociology, and gerontology. Wandering around the great university filled with rich research opportunities and those who aspired to advance their field, I soon realized my desired goal was clinical psychology and that I, too, might one day find my niche. Although I minored in gerontology and hoped to focus more on the aging population in graduate school, it was not to be. Fate would intervene and soon determine my future path and clinical interest.

I began my graduate training at a small Catholic institution in clinical psychology. As part of the curriculum, I learned the different schools of psychotherapy (e.g., CBT, psychodynamic, experiential), and then as a practicum student I learned how to apply them to my first clients. CBT emerged as my early favorite, and it seemed initially that each client, regardless of diagnosis or personality, was suited for it. I remember using technical words like *cognitive restructuring* and *thought stopping* but never words to describe the clients' needs and preferences. I do not even recall asking clients what *they* wanted out of therapy. I assumed after a lengthy intake (three to five sessions) that I (or my supervisor) knew best. I would ask clients what they wanted in terms of treatment goals but most were unsure how to *operationally define* (another term my graduate program loved) them. I never asked clients if they thought therapy was working for them nor did I ask if they were happy with the treatment they were receiving. It never occurred to me and was never mentioned by my supervisors. How unfortunate for them and for me.

I got married and had back-to-back girls 13 months apart, at which point I changed my status to a half-time PsyD student. After considering

only community placements within a 30-mile radius of home, I landed my first practicum at the counseling center at my institution. Never before had I considered working with a college student population, but I found a true passion once I began. This was also the first time I received supervision outside my graduate program. After taking 4.5 years off to be with my children, I was fortunate to find a local, half-time internship at the University of Scranton counseling center and again worked with college students. I stayed on as a part-time postdoctoral resident and was offered a position upon completion.

During the fourth year of my doctoral program, I completed a course in clinical supervision. The course acquainted me with the fundamentals of the enterprise, and I even co-supervised a couple of graduate students in their first and second years of study. Alas, the course also left me feeling lost and alone, lacking any meaningful structure for conducting supervision or, for that matter, performing psychotherapy.

With clinical experience and a change to an integrative supervisor, I began to realize that CBT or any monotherapy was not the way to go. In fact, I needed and desired systematic integration. The more freedom I had to be myself and to systemically tailor therapy to the entire client, the more skilled and comfortable I became. And once I found the integrative path, there was no turning back.

The process of integration was transparent for both my clients and me. I found that using the stages of change was indispensable during treatment planning and a much better alternative to expressing my frustration with certain clients during supervision. JCN encouraged me to treat each client individually using multiple methods adapted to his or her stages and preferences for session frequency, therapist directiveness, outside-therapy work, and the like. Although in the beginning, the process felt as though I was checking off a list of questions, it quickly became part of my intake session. Most important, it worked! I began to rely on the research evidence in selecting clinical methods and in constructing a personalized therapeutic relationship. JCN taught me to conduct serial assessments to track clients' progress and to obtain feedback from them to ensure they were satisfied with our work. I was

empowered by JCN to be my own advocate and, likewise, encourage my clients to advocate on their own behalf. Integration simultaneously fit me and my clients.

Integrative supervision has catapulted my own desire to supervise. As someone at the end of her "official" training, I find myself conflicted. I am ready to leave the nest yet afraid to take that first leap. Supervision goes quickly, and I find myself wishing I could go back in time to restart the experience (of course, knowing what I know now!).

## ROAD MAP FOR THIS BOOK

In this opening chapter, we have introduced psychotherapy integration, broadly defined *supervision*, and provided historical background on integrative supervision. We outlined a personal and professional path to becoming an expert integrative supervisor.

In Chapter 2, we focus on essential dimensions of integrative supervision: its critical goals, unique functions, and the supervisory relationship. We briefly touch on the negative effects of a poor supervisory relationship, as it accounts for the majority of damaging supervision experiences. Without a trusting, respectful, and caring relationship, not much of value seems to transpire in supervision. We discuss the need for routine bilateral evaluation of both the supervisee and the supervisor.

Chapter 3 leads you through the multiple methods of integrative supervision, such as video recording, process notes, documentation, and parallel process. The distinctive aspect of integrative supervision is its tailoring supervision to the unique supervisee just as that supervisee is simultaneously tailoring treatment to his or her unique client. We review the meta-analytic evidence for doing so and its documented success for all parties in the supervisory triad (supervisor, supervisee, patient).

Chapter 4 gets to the nuts and bolts of integrative supervision. We offer an insider's look into what actually transpires in our typical supervision sessions via verbatim transcripts from multiple sessions. We selected excerpts that best represent integrative supervision and what distinguishes it from other types of supervision.

Chapter 5 takes you through some common supervisory dilemmas. These include supervisory conflicts and their resolution, difficult supervisees, supervisee deficits, power differentials, multicultural conflicts, and legal and ethical conflicts. Psychotherapists suffer from high levels of brownout and burnout, so in the following chapter we focus on self-care for both the supervisor and the supervisee.

In Chapter 7, we barrage you with the research support for integrative supervision. Exciting research suggests that integrative supervision outperforms supervision as usual. In the final chapter, we consider probable future directions for clinical supervision in general and the integrative approach in particular. The book concludes with our recommended readings on integrative supervision.

We have genuinely enjoyed working on the APA supervision video series and this book, *Supervision Essentials for Integrative Psychotherapy*. Our fervent goals are to broaden the scope of typical supervision, demonstrate the documented benefits of integrative supervision, help diffuse any fears that it is "too damn hard," and encourage others to join the integrative path. Although integration does not prove easy or useful for all contexts, one soon discovers its numerous advantages for supervisees and supervisors alike. And, in the end of course, it's all about improved care, and integrative supervision appears to be producing improved outcomes for clients. In the words of one sagacious trainee, "The benefits of integration far outweigh any struggles in learning the approach."

# Key Principles

Integrative supervision leverages multiple theoretical orientations and accumulated research evidence to fit individual trainees in ways that improve their clinical skills and thereby enhance the clinical outcomes of their patients. This type of supervision entails a deliberate parallel process: customizing supervision to trainees while trainees simultaneously customize psychological methods and therapeutic relationships to the specific and varied needs of individual patients. The aim of such a systematic, research-informed supervision is a more efficient and efficacious therapy that fits both the client and the supervisee–clinician.

We are committed to the integrative approach but do not insist that our supervisees adopt this approach for themselves. Most do, but not all. Our intention is not necessarily to produce "card carrying, flag waving" integrative psychotherapists (Beutler et al., 1987). This scenario would simply replace enforced commitment to a single system with enforced

http://dx.doi.org/10.1037/15967-002
*Supervision Essentials for Integrative Psychotherapy*, by J. C. Norcross and L. M. Popple
Copyright © 2017 by the American Psychological Association. All rights reserved.

conversion to an integrative system, a change that may be more pluralistic and liberating in content but certainly not in process. Rather, our goal is to assist supervisees in thinking and behaving integratively—openly, creatively, and synthetically in accord with the research (Norcross, Beutler, & Clarkin, 1990). An informed pluralism, a critical relativism in supervision will eventually afford us—and our patients—the greatest returns.

In this chapter, we unpack these key principles: supervision goals, tasks, expectations, relationships, evaluations, and feedback. Page limitations drive us to focus on what is distinctive about integrative supervision throughout.

## GOALS

A fascinating, albeit taxing, feature of clinical supervision is its multiple goals. The APA (2015) guidelines define supervision as a distinct professional practice "which has the goals of enhancing the professional competence and science-informed practice of the supervisee, monitoring the quality of services provided, protecting the public, and providing a gatekeeping function for entry into the profession." That's four ambitious and occasionally conflicting goals.

Let's begin with the primary goal in mind: Grow the trainee to think and practice integratively in ways that increase the effectiveness of clinical services. What are the supervisory experiences, methods, and relationships that promote that end? We ambitiously strive to expand the minds and repertoires of supervisees. As Oliver Wendell Holmes, Sr. once wrote, "The mind, once expanded to the dimensions of larger ideas, never returns to its original size."

Supervision goals depend in large part on the nature of the clinical training in which the supervision is embedded. The major choice is whether the objective of the supervision is to train students to competence in a single psychotherapy system and subsequent referral of some clients to more appropriate treatments, or whether the objective is for trainees to accommodate most of these clients themselves by virtue of their competence in multimethod, multimodality psychotherapy

(Norcross et al., 1990). Either integrative alternative probably constitutes an improvement over current training paradigms.

## Single-System Competence and Systematic Referral

A modest but still significantly integrative objective in supervision is to ensure students' competence in a single therapy system—for example, psychodynamic, cognitive, or experiential—for those clients and problems for whom that therapy system is indicated and then ensure their ability to make systematic referrals for clients and problems for which that therapy system is contraindicated. Mental health professionals can function effectively in a single and comfortable theoretical system provided they have the ethics and talent to discriminate which clients can optimally benefit from their preferred system and which cannot. Referral of the latter group of clients can then systematically be made to clinicians competent to offer the indicated service.

The two essential tasks for the supervisor here are to train students to recognize the respective contraindications in their single theory and to educate them in making informed referral decisions. Helping single-system advocates to relinquish clients for whom another approach is better suited will entail attention to both the prescriptions of the empirical research and the limitations of their theoretical commitments (Norcross et al., 1990). We return to this sticky matter in a later chapter on handling common supervisory challenges because some trainees are convinced, despite the mountain of research evidence, that their preferred therapy will optimally benefit all patients and problems.

Many therapy supervisors routinely adhere to such an approach without recognizing its integrative objectives. Frequently the "treatment of choice" is one associated with a particular brand of therapy, such as exposure therapy for panic disorder, or conjoint sessions for couple conflict, or insight-oriented therapy for personality disorders. The clinical and ethical concern is not from narrow-gauge therapists per se but from therapists who impose that narrowness on their clients (Stricker, 1988).

Furthermore, competence in pure-form or single-theory psychotherapies is a necessary prerequisite to integration, which relies on the constituent elements provided by the respective brand-name therapies—the clinical methods, the interpersonal stances, and the research findings. Students will rely on single-system therapies in reaching their integration; after all, one cannot integrate what one does not know.

This supervision goal, in our experience, is clearly indicated for trainees enrolled in most master's programs, which accept an average of 60% to 70% of applicants (Norcross & Sayette, 2016), many of whom do not possess substantial undergraduate course work or clinical experience in the anticipated profession. To be sure, students learn the value of integration in their graduate course work. But a couple of practica will not suffice to ensure competence in several systems of psychotherapy. At the end of a master's degree, it is probably best to become a master of one system rather than a jack of all trades and competent in none.

## Integrative Practice

A broader and more ambitious undertaking in supervision is to aim for student competence in integrative psychotherapy wherein the student provides indicated treatment for most clients. Of critical importance to this decision is the assumption that students can learn to practice several models and multiple methods competently. Plentiful evidence has accumulated to demonstrate that it is possible for a given therapist to selectively apply in an effective way methods drawn from different perspectives. Doctoral programs—by virtue of their lengthier training, more stringent admission requirements, and insistence on prerequisite course work in the field—are the most likely venues for this type of training. Our experiences in doctoral-level psychology and psychiatry programs over the past 3 decades affirm the probability of producing competent integrative psychotherapists, although additional effort is typically required in light of the ambitious training goal.

The remainder of this volume focuses on this more ambitious and time-consuming goal of supervision. We are mindful that this goal rarely

proves possible during master's programs, but committed psychotherapists learn throughout their careers. Many, as did LMP, come to integration after their graduate training.

## Optimal Timing for Integrative Supervision

Choosing between single-system competence and systematic referral on the one hand and competence in integrative psychotherapy on the other depends in part on the temporal sequence of students' professional development. As beginners, most psychotherapists seek out a single theory by which they can define themselves, manage their anxiety, and solidify their identity. Ideological singularity often serves as a defense against clinical complexity (Schultz-Ross, 1995). Beginners feel a naïve sense of security in adhering to the methods of a single orientation; however, such reassurance is inevitably short-lived as they come to realize the clinical limitations of any singular approach. If we manualize anything, it should be flexibility and effectiveness (Beutler, 1999).

The early and strong consensus is that the sophisticated adoption of an integrative perspective occurs after learning specific therapy systems and their attendant methods (e.g., Andrews, Norcross, & Halgin, 1992; Beutler et al., 1987; Halgin, 1988; Norcross et al., 1986). Thus, at the beginning of graduate work, supervision would focus primarily on competence in a single system of therapy and systematic referral, whereas in the later stages of professional development, supervision would opt for integrative practice. Integrative psychotherapy probably mandates greater levels of cognitive complexity, clinical experience, and tolerance for ambiguity in its practitioners.

However, that does not imply that integration should wait until late in the training or supervision sequence (Ziv-Beiman, 2014). On the contrary, from the beginning, students should be exposed to all therapeutic approaches with minimal judgment being made as to their relative contributions to truth. Theoretical paradigms would be introduced as tentative and explanatory notions, varying in level of experience, goals, and methodology. Multiple systems of psychotherapy would be presented critically

but within a paradigm of comparison and integration (Prochaska & Norcross, 2013). Integrative frameworks and informed pluralism would thereby be introduced at the beginning of training (Halgin, 1985), but formal integrative supervision would typically occur later in the sequence.

*Deep structure* integration will take considerable time and probably come about only after the therapist has had years of clinical experience (Messer, 1992). Expert psychotherapists represent their domain on a semantically and conceptually deeper level than do novices. Conceptual learning about psychotherapy integration is probably necessary to achieve deep integration but is not sufficient. For therapists to integrate at a deeper level requires that they first understand and integrate within each individual therapy and only then across therapies. Clinical experience and disciplined reflection on that experience are needed to attain a mature synthesis.

Integration, in other words, may take two broad forms that are differentially accessible to novice versus expert therapists (Schacht, 1991). The first form, accessible to neophytes, emphasizes conceptual products that enter the educational arena as content additions to the curriculum. The second form of integration, largely limited to more experienced therapists, emphasizes a special mode of thinking. This form enters the educational arena through accumulated and supervised experiences that promote fluent performance and creative metacognitive skills.

In our minds, integrative supervision assumes that the trainee has been exposed to the range of theories and techniques, has at least 2 years of clinical experience, and has acquired nascent competence in at least one system of therapy. Then, with a rudimentary understanding of differential treatment selection, integrative supervision profitably ensues.

## What Is Integrated?

For the sake of simplicity and of comparability with the other books in this series, we address primarily the integration of diverse systems of psychotherapy. However, integrative treatment planning is far more comprehensive and complex than the blending of techniques or theories.

Integrative formulation and planning constitute a series of sequential, cascading decisions across multiple domains: whether to offer treatment, the treatment setting, therapy intensity, clinical formats, relationship qualities, the value of pharmacotherapy, and, of course, the choice of strategies and techniques (Beutler, Clarkin, & Bongar, 2000). 'Tis a complex, recursive decisional matrix of what is the best treatment for this particular patient.

In that regard, one routinely encounters references in the literature and in the classroom to integrating self-help and psychotherapy, integrating research and practice, integrating Western and Eastern perspectives, integrating social advocacy with psychotherapy, and so on. All are indeed laudable pursuits, but we restrict ourselves in this volume to the traditional meaning of integration as the blending of diverse theoretical orientations.

## TASKS AND FUNCTIONS

A supervisor can flexibly and fruitfully move among the roles of lecturer, teacher, case reviewer, collegial peer, monitor, advocate, mentor, and quasi-therapist throughout the course of one meeting or over many supervision contacts (Hess, 1980). In the teaching literature, this ability to balance a trusting, supportive relationship with the evaluative function (assigning grades, offering corrective feedback) has been characterized as cheerleading versus gatekeeping. In addition to these common roles, we identify several other functions relatively specific to integrative supervisors.

### Cultivating Respect for Research

Interlacing practice and science during training will yield a generation of therapists who are more inclined to rely on outcome research than on theoretical narcissism in selecting clinical methods and interpersonal stances for specific patients (Meltzoff, 1984). The net result of integrative supervision, we hope, will be knowledgeable psychotherapists who will approach patients with an open mind, an empirical disposition, and a

relentless commitment to customize their interventions to the inevitable complexities of human behavior.

Toward that end, we recommend multiple readings for supervisees on "what works" and on what is most likely to work for a given patient. If trainees are not already familiar, we introduce them to compilations of evidence-based assessments, methods, principles, relationships, and self-help (e.g., Castonguay & Beutler, 2017; Hunsley & Marsh, 2008; Nathan & Gorman, 2015; Norcross, 2011; Norcross, Campbell, et al., 2013). Because those compilations mature and evolve, we familiarize trainees with a process of efficiently scanning the knowledge base for effective methods by using a sequence of core evidence-based practice skills. One helpful mnemonic (Norcross, Hogan, Koocher, & Maggio, 2017) is AAA TIE (can be pronounced "triple A tie"):

1. Asking a specific, clinical question.
2. Accessing the best available research.
3. Appraising critically that research evidence.
4. Translating that research into practice with a particular patient.
5. Integrating the clinician's expertise and patient's characteristics, culture, and preferences with the research.
6. Evaluating the effectiveness of the entire process.

## Assessing Transdiagnostic Patient Features

Psychotherapy has matured to the point where treatment selection can be largely based on indications and contraindications culled from the comparative outcome research. Thus, a central task of supervision is to assist trainees in collecting sufficient information on these multiple client markers to select and implement the indicated change strategies. These strategies, you will recall, concern not only treatment methods but also the assessment procedures, the therapy relationship, the treatment format, and the like.

Typically, integrative supervisors strongly value clinical assessment that guides effective treatment. Such assessment is conducted early in psychotherapy to select treatment methods and therapy relationships that

are most likely to be effective, throughout therapy to monitor the patient's response and to make midcourse adjustments as needed, and toward the end of psychotherapy to evaluate the outcomes of the entire enterprise. Thus, assessment is continuous and collaborative.

Supervising clinical assessment of the patient is relatively traditional, with one major exception. The assessment interviews entail collecting information on presenting problems, relevant histories, and treatment expectations and goals as well as building a working alliance. As psychologists, we also typically employ psychological testing as a means of securing additional data and identifying clinical and personality disorders. We recommend both symptomatic rating forms (e.g., Beck Depression Inventory-II, Symptom Checklist-90-Revised) and broader measures of pathology and personality (e.g., Minnesota Multiphasic Personality Inventory—II, Millon Clinical Multiaxial Inventory—III).

The one way in which assessment for integrative work departs from the usual is that we collect information on multiple patient dimensions that will guide treatment selection. In fact, quick in-session assessments and/or computer-based assessments for clients enhance the development of treatment plans. Because there are thousands of potential combinations of patient, therapist, treatment, and setting variables that could contribute, we rely primarily on the empirical research (as outlined below) to identify a limited number of patient dimensions that influence therapy success, and we supervise students in using focused assessments on those dimensions that are most predictive of differential treatment response.

Integrative supervision thus provides guidance on assessment of diagnostic and especially transdiagnostic patient markers at the onset of psychotherapy. It is, according to Sir William Osler (1906), the father of modern medicine, "much more important to know what sort of a patient has a disease than what sort of disease a patient has." At least seven robust patient features suggest a particular treatment and relational tack as judged by meta-analyses: primary diagnosis, treatment goal, reactance level, stage of change, coping style, culture, and preferences. In our experience, a 1-year (50-session) course of individual supervision usually manages to cover four of these features and assist supervisees in acquiring comfort

and competence in assessing them in routine practice. The supervisor's task, then, is to instruct, coach, and practice efficient means to accurately assess the patient dimensions most relevant to the case at hand and to the supervisee's needs and settings.

## Implementing Integrative Therapies

Once supervisees have collected sufficient information on these transdiagnostic patient markers, the supervisory task becomes assisting trainees to implement the indicated treatment methods and interpersonal stances. Herewith is a précis on the meta-analytic research and indicated differential responses for several of these patient–treatment fits (for a full review, consult the meta-analyses in Norcross, 2011).

### *Reactance Level*

Reactance is a stable personality trait that refers to being easily provoked and responding oppositionally to external demands. It exists on a normally distributed continuum of compliance (low) to defiance (high). As expected, high patient reactance or resistance is consistently associated with poorer therapy outcomes (in 82% of studies), but matching therapist directiveness to client reactance mightily improves therapy outcome. Specifically, clients presenting with high reactance benefit more from self-control methods, minimal therapist directiveness, and paradoxical interventions. By contrast, clients with low reactance benefit more from therapist directiveness and explicit guidance. This strong, consistent finding can be expressed as a large effect size ($d$) averaging 0.76 (Beutler, Harwood, Michelson, Song, & Holman, 2011). How directive might an optimally effective supervisee be? It depends upon the patient, specifically his or her reactance level.

### *Stages of Change*

As also expected, the amount of progress clients make in psychotherapy tends to be a direct function of their pretreatment stage of change—precontemplation, contemplation, preparation, action, and maintenance.

A meta-analysis of 39 psychotherapy studies (Norcross, Krebs, & Prochaska, 2011) found a mean effect size ($d$) of 0.46, indicating that the stages reliably predict outcomes in psychotherapy.

More important, research in behavioral medicine and psychotherapy converges in showing that different processes of change are differentially effective in certain stages of change. A meta-analysis (Rosen, 2000) of 47 studies examining the relationships among the stages and the processes of change showed large effect sizes ($d$ = 0.70 and 0.80); that is, adapting psychotherapy to the client's stage of change significantly improves outcome across disorders (Prochaska & Norcross, 2013). Action-oriented therapies are quite effective with individuals who are in the preparation or action stages. However, these same therapies tend to be less effective or even detrimental with individuals in the precontemplation and contemplation stages.

## Coping Style

The research has been devoted primarily to the externalizing (impulsive, stimulation-seeking, extroverted) and internalizing (self-critical, inhibited, introverted) coping styles. Approximately 80% of the studies investigating this dimension have demonstrated differential effects of treatment type as a function of patient coping style. A meta-analysis of 12 of those studies, involving more than 1,000 patients, revealed a medium effect ($d$ = 0.55) for matching therapist method to patient coping style (Beutler et al., 2011). Interpersonal and insight-oriented therapies are more effective among internalizing patients, whereas symptom-focused and skill-building therapies are more effective among externalizing patients. This pattern is frequently known for child patients—say, a depressed internalizing girl versus a hyperactive externalizing boy—but less well known for the adult patients on whom the meta-analyses were conducted.

## Preferences

Treatment goals specify what is to be accomplished; preferences, by contrast, specify how those goals might be best accomplished. Patient

preferences can frequently serve as direct indicators of the best therapeutic method and healing relationship for that person. Decades of empirical evidence attest to the benefit of seriously considering, and at least beginning with, the relational and treatment preferences of the client. A meta-analysis of 35 studies compared the treatment outcomes of clients matched to their preferred treatment to outcomes of those clients not matched to their preference. The findings indicate a medium positive effect ($d = 0.31$) in favor of clients matched to preferences. Clients who were matched to their preference were one-third less likely to drop out of psychotherapy—a powerful effect indeed (Swift, Callahan, & Vollmer, 2011).

A transcript of a supervision session presented later in this book, in which we discuss termination with a client, brings this point home to both supervisor and supervisee. In a termination session, the client addresses the power of preferences. The client informs the supervisee–therapist (LMP) that had she not accommodated his preferences, he would have ceased treatment.

### Culture

A meta-analysis of 65 studies, encompassing 8,620 clients, evaluated the effectiveness of culturally adapted therapies versus traditional, nonadapted therapies. The most frequent methods of adaptation in the studies involved incorporating cultural content and values, using the client's preferred language, and matching therapists of similar ethnicity. The results revealed a positive effect ($d = 0.46$) in favor of clients receiving culturally adapted treatments (Smith, Rodriguez, & Bernal, 2011). Cultural "fit" works, not only as an ethical commitment but also as an evidence-based practice.

These client markers provide prescriptive as well as proscriptive guidance, requiring use of a variety of treatment methods and interpersonal stances. In reactance, for instance, the prescriptive implication is to match the therapist's amount of directiveness to the patient's reactance. The proscriptive implications entail avoiding meeting high client reactance with high therapist direction and, less likely, meeting low client reactance with low therapist direction.

Trainees enter supervision with their own personalities, preferences, and prior experiences, of course. These seem to accommodate client needs perhaps half the time. Helping them offer at other times what is most effective for their clients, versus what is most comfortable for themselves, occupies a considerable portion of supervision time.

All told, these responsive fits to the entirety of the patient prove far more powerful than the historical match of Treatment Method A to Disorder Z. As just seen, the typical effect sizes for customizing to these transdiagnostic features are in the 0.50 to 0.80 range, whereas the differential effects of a particular treatment method to a particular disorder fall between 0 (the equivalent outcomes of the dodo bird) and at best 0.20 (Wampold & Imel, 2015).

## Promoting and Tracking the Relationship

These large effect sizes for adapting psychotherapy to the individual client rival the powerful effects of the therapeutic relationship, except the latter is largely correlational research and the customizing or treatment–patient fit studies are controlled and experimental, which enable causal conclusions.

Virtually all supervisors and supervisees will claim, and genuinely believe, that they offer strong supervisory and therapeutic relationships, as do virtually all integrative supervisors. The important twists are that many integrative supervisors (a) concretely identify what works in those relationships, (b) formally track their purportedly strong relationships, and (c) tailor those relationships specifically to the other person. We will have more to say about these elements later in the book, but for now we offer a few words on each fairly distinctive departure from the usual way of working with both the therapeutic relationship and the supervisory relationship.

I (JCN) frequently ask supervisees to specify which of their behaviors are especially helpful to the therapeutic relationship. In my experience, they are often mystified by this request and typically gurgle the Rogerian facilitative conditions or "the alliance." We help them build on their

responses in supervision and carefully cultivate those relational behaviors that have been shown to work in the meta-analytic research (Norcross, 2011). These include, inter alia,

- the alliance in youth and adult therapy: an emergent partnership between therapist and client, built principally on a positive emotional bond between therapist and client, and their ability to agree on the goals of treatment and to reach a mutual consensus on the tasks (Horvath, Del Re, Flückiger, & Symonds, 2011; Shirk & Karver, 2011);
- the alliance in couple and family therapy (Friedlander, Escudero, Heatherington, & Diamond, 2011);
- cohesion in group therapy (Burlingame, McClendon, & Alonso, 2011);
- empathy (Elliott, Bohart, Watson, & Greenberg, 2011);
- goal consensus (Tryon & Winograd, 2011);
- collaboration (Tryon & Winograd, 2011);
- affirmation/positive regard (Farber & Doolin, 2011); and
- repairing alliance ruptures (Safran, Muran, & Eubanks-Carter, 2011).

Although researchers cannot study all of these relationship behaviors simultaneously and there is considerable overlap in these constructs, it is demonstrably true that these relationship behaviors are important predictors of and contributors to psychotherapy success. More important for supervision, they can be identified, taught to a large degree, and cultivated within the supervision session. As well, these behaviors are instrumental in creating and maintaining a strong supervisory relationship.

Many students entering supervision assume rather than document that their relationships with clients are exceptionally positive. Similarly, many fellow supervisors inform us that their first and principal task is to create a solid alliance with their supervisees. However, these statements are rarely documented or evaluated in a formal manner. In our integrative supervision, we prefer to explicitly track the status and progress of these relationships in session.

We ask that supervisees periodically collect feedback from their clients, and as supervisors we do likewise. The supervisee systematically monitors a client's mental health vital signs through the use of standardized scales

and expected treatment response. Results of this monitoring are then fed back in real time to the supervisee and discussed in session with the client.

A meta-analysis of nine studies on the impact of feedback methods on treatment outcomes showed effect sizes ($d$) between 0.49 and 0.70 (Lambert & Shimokawa, 2011). Rates of patient deterioration in psychotherapy were cut by two-thirds when client feedback was used with warning signals for at-risk patients. Such monitoring leads to increased opportunities to repair alliance ruptures, enhance motivation, and reduce premature termination. Systematic feedback is especially useful in helping supervisees identify the possible failure of ongoing treatment and collaborate with the client in restoring positive outcomes.

At least 10 feedback systems are now available for routine practice (see Hilsenroth, 2015), and dozens of supervisory relationship questionnaires have been published (see appendices in Bernard & Goodyear, 2014). We explain and illustrate with a transcript our preferred means of doing so in a subsequent section.

Last, integrative supervision probably differs from most forms of supervision by adapting the supervisory relationship to more supervisee characteristics, not only to the client's diagnosis/problem list or the supervisee's experience level but to the entirety of the supervisee—stage of change, reactance level, culture, and so on. Recall that the ultimate objective of integrative supervision is to tailor the supervision approach to individual trainees in ways to enhance the outcome of both their clients and their competence. (Just a teaser of sorts here; more on tailoring supervision to individual differences in the next chapter.)

## Understanding and Managing Supervisee Consternation

Early in supervision contacts, beginning with the initial meeting, we raise the supervisee's probable consternations about undertaking integrative work. This constitutes a core and distinctive task of integrative supervision.

Heide and Rosenbaum (1988) surveyed 14 psychotherapists regarding their experiences in using single versus combined theoretical models

in psychotherapy; their results nicely anticipate our trainees' frequent concerns. Contrary to predictions, the two conditions did not differ in self-reported supervisee anxiety. However, when using a single orientation, psychotherapists reported being significantly more self-controlled, conventional, precise, and reserved. When using a combined or integrative model, they said they were more imaginative, adventuresome, spontaneous, and changeable. That's also our take on integrative supervision: more imaginative, adventuresome, and changeable—and more effective.

But if the clash of theoretical persuasions rings of adventure, it also sounds like occasional disequilibrium. We will phrase several of these sources of disequilibrium in the way we often hear them: as anxious threats to therapeutic identity and competence (Norcross, 1990).

- *"But which of these many paths shall I take at any one point?"* Should the student promote action or explore mental content; challenge or understand irrational cognitions; work on actual or projected relationships; or empathize or redirect during a session (Messer, 1992)? Of course, these choices are not as dualistic, either/or, as they are phrased. Nevertheless, the change in style implies a change in identity, a transformation of sorts (Rosenbaum, 1988). Both integrative supervision and integrative practice entail shifts within a single session, across many sessions with the same person, or between sessions with different people. The result can be anxiety and perplexity, occasionally articulated but more frequently not. These concerns diminish in a few weeks once supervisees understand that there is a systematic, research-informed structure to treatment selection.
- *"It is just too damn hard!"* Students and supervisors alike complain of additional work and of increased mental effort. Not dissimilar to switch hitters in baseball and bilingual children, the participants in integrative supervision pull double duty in the short run for more flexible and comprehensive skills in the long run.
- *"If today is Wednesday and it's 5 p.m., then this must be cognitive-behavioral therapy!"* Akin to those whirlwind European tours, frequent visits to diverse therapeutic communities require considerable physical stamina and mental preparation.

- *"Oh, I don't like doing this type of psychotherapy!"* Therapists are not as personally attached or psychologically comfortable with some therapies as they are with other therapies, even controlling for competence in them. Several psychotherapeutic methods and relationships simply don't "fit" supervisees. Thus, they may be asked to adopt a relationship stance or conduct a treatment method indicated for a given client even though they don't particularly enjoy it.
- *"I am becoming a jack of all trades, master of none."* This cited disadvantage of integration (Norcross & Prochaska, 1988) is not an identity we eagerly embrace but is one that, like many stereotypes, has a grain of truth to it. This concerns the inherent conflict between depth and breadth. An indisputable disadvantage of aiming to establish multiple competences is that it will necessitate longer and more comprehensive training than will a single competency. When supervisees are delayed in acquiring competence in multiple methods of psychotherapy, they are apt to feel more frustrated. The future promises of increased efficacy and applicability as a result of integrative therapy hold more appeal for supervisors than for supervisees at times.
- *"I am opening myself up here to chaos! Who knows what can happen."* The ambiguity and uncertainty of differential practice can be emotionally taxing (even as it is exciting and spontaneous). Clinical experiences will not be as predictable and controlled as a pure-form therapy practiced uniformly. Supervisees may be dismayed that their own attempts might prove to be awkward and disruptive (Wachtel, 1991).

In broader strokes, these and other liabilities highlight two central matters regarding integrative supervision. First, such practice and supervision engender a rich variety of countertransferential reactions and can exact a toll on the clinician (Halgin & McEntee, 1993). Integrative practices—"when worlds collide"—offer fertile ground for the generation of emotional responses, even in its proponents. Second, the decision to opt for integrative supervision requires a cost–benefit analysis—the intellectual challenge versus the internal conflicts, the gratifying openness versus the anxious ambiguity—that is part and parcel of the process of integration. That's also the reasoning behind our insistence that integrative supervision

be reserved for trainees already exposed to a range of theories and techniques and having at least 2 years of clinical experience and nascent competence in at least one system of therapy. The integrative journey is arduous; it is unrealistic to expect beginners to competently plunge into integrative work early in their development. Integrative supervision should not be tried at home or with beginners!

## SETTING EXPECTATIONS

Much as we insist on our trainees identifying the relative indications and contraindications of treatment options for their clients, we are equally adamant about identifying the indications and contraindications of integrative supervision. This is not to say that integrative approaches possess an inordinate number of limitations but rather that we endeavor to model an informed pluralism toward our own work. Such openness about the strengths and liabilities of integrative supervision, as posed by its practitioners (supervisors) and its recipients (supervisees), sets clear expectations from the beginning. That style, we trust, is manifested early in supervision sessions by understanding and managing supervisee consternations, as just described.

The difficulty of becoming a "good" supervisee is oft neglected. Trainees usually enter supervision with little understanding of the process, and they often do not receive formal assistance in assuming the role of supervisee. Both of us confess to being fairly clueless on how to avail ourselves as supervisees at first. It should come as no surprise that supervisee ratings and faculty/expert ratings of the quality of the same supervision session evince quite low correlations (e.g., Bernard & Goodyear, 2014; Reichelt & Skjerve, 2002; Shanfield, Hetherly, & Matthews, 2001). Many supervisor and supervisee dyads are literally not on the same page.

Psychotherapy supervision, particularly of the integrative variety, requires formal preparation of students and structured orientation to supervision (Berger & Buchholz, 1993). Such an orientation addresses the participants' goals and expectations, the logistics of supervision (e.g., setting, format, boundaries, legal relationship), and its omnipresent evaluative

component (e.g., grading criteria, course credit, letters of recommendations). In fact, we are among those who opt for an explicit contract for supervision.

Following the initial sessions of two new supervision relationships, I (JCN) recently jotted down notes on their content and process as we set expectations. The content seemed to heavily rely on mutually reviewing and editing a written supervision agreement. So we begin there in this section, then move on to matters more concerned with the process.

## Written Contracts

In years past, I (JCN) was reluctant to commit supervisory agreements to paper as I found that a bit legalistic and over the top. In recent years, perhaps owing to my age, experience, or timidity related to the legal atmosphere in which we operate, I have gotten it in writing.

In any case, clinical experience and supervision research highlight the importance of sharing perceptions of the supervision relationship. Mutual failures in a supervisory relationship can often be attributed to discrepant perceptions of each other and appropriate roles. Written contracts clarify expectations, set goals, and reduce misperceptions. I (JCN) employ a four-page, single-spaced generic supervision contract reviewed and individualized with each supervisee. Parts and phrases were adapted from half a dozen published sources, and the contract contains the usual explicit sections on interpersonal roles, attendance expectations, evaluation methods, and provisions for revising the contract. The supervisee and supervisor walk through the document together, refining the contents and editing as necessary. We then sign and date the agreement.

Nothing in the agreement strikes us as particularly novel, but supervisees do comment frequently on a few matters. For one, I ask supervisees to bring treatment notes for the past week on clients to be discussed for review in the supervision session. I do so for all clients of beginning clinicians but only for some clients of more advanced trainees. For another, the agreement stipulates that the evaluation feedback will be bidirectional—how the supervisor can improve and how the supervisee can improve.

For still another, some supervisees are surprised by a sentence in the agreement that reads, "The supervisor expects the supervisee to express disagreements in opinion and to discuss any conflicts in the supervisory relationship."

Although I (LMP), as a supervisee, had supervision contracts before, they were not tailored specifically to me and never did I and my supervisor review them together before I began supervision. A bit intimidating and a tad legalistic initially, the contract constituted my first peek through the door to integrative supervision. My input was requested, and I was encouraged to be honest about my learning needs and goals. I found it was not just talk. JCN meant what he said when he requested bidirectional feedback and discussions of conflict. Although completing the contract took an entire supervision hour, once it was finished we never needed to look at it again. A contract that explicitly stated expectations of both parties would have been a respite in past supervisory experiences.

## Process Matters

One of my (JCN) favorite expressions in supervision is "process matters"—meaning that we want to achieve the stated goals on the contract, of course, but how we relate and get to those goals matter as well. I ask, on the contract and in person, for supervisee self-reflection, honesty, continuing evaluation of their performance, feedback on my functioning, and lots of reading.

Compared with other supervisors, I (JCN) am repeatedly apprised that I request more readings. Advanced trainees are asked to read one of my publications on integrative supervision and another on how I came to integration (Norcross, 2006). Novice supervisees, or those without much experience in adopting a productive supervisee role, skim the book, *Getting the Most Out of Clinical Training and Supervision* (Falender & Shafranske, 2011). Supervisees then read about the particular treatment methods, relationship stances, and patient transdiagnostic features; doing so means that they will consult multiple treatment manuals, websites, and compilations. Supervisees also watch multiple video recordings of expert

therapists demonstrating treatments and relationships. Most of these are drawn from the APA Psychotherapy Video Series, which has blossomed into the largest—with more than 125 individual demonstration sessions and more than 25 six-session demonstration sets—and arguably most influential psychotherapy video series in the world (Norcross & VandenBos, 2011). Research generally demonstrates that watching video recordings produces improvements in learning specific therapy skills (e.g., Maguire et al., 1984) and even entire psychotherapy systems (e.g., Hilsenroth, Defife, Blagys, & Ackerman, 2006).

The process of setting expectations includes the supervisor sharing his or her own work and follies. An early couples therapy supervisor (Jim Prochaska) played an audiotape of his first effort at conjoint marital therapy during the first meeting of our group supervision. The taped session disintegrated within 10 minutes, punctuated by the marital partners screaming at each other, a weak therapist offering ineffective suggestions, and the couple storming out of the session. Our supervisor then looked at us and said, "You will all do better than I did." To this day, I try to show examples of my therapeutic blunders—an empathic failure, a dumb-ass comment, a forgotten piece of crucial patient information, my hastily scrawled session note that communicates nothing of import. As supervision proceeds, I might suggest that supervisees watch a published video recording of me conducting psychotherapy, but that can prompt unfavorable comparisons to their own work.

How does the supervisee best accept feedback? That's a common query that sets supervision expectations (feedback will be forthcoming) and reflects our emphasis on tailoring supervision (and therapy) to the individual. Supervisees seem taken aback by the question, probably owing to its rarity, its directness, and its responsiveness. Sometimes I ask how that feedback should be tailored to them on a 10-point veritas (blunt truth) to gravitas (virtuous support) scale. For the anxious beginning supervisee, we might respectfully ask, "How can you feel trusting here? How can this be a safe learning place?" Such exchanges create the mental and interpersonal set for integrative supervision.

## ROLE OF RELATIONSHIP

It is curious and perhaps paradoxical to write about the role of the relationship in clinical supervision when supervision *is* a relationship! If not the entirety of supervision, the relationship is at least its heart and soul (Watkins, 2014). In the words of Hanna Levenson paraphrasing Fiscalini (1985), "Supervision is a relationship about a relationship about other relationships." The supervisory relationship—like the therapeutic relationship—is the key mechanism of change and exhibits the highest correlations to supervisees' reports of effective clinical supervision (M. V. Ellis, 2010). Supervision occurs within, by, and through the relationship; maps and methods can facilitate the journey, but ultimately success depends largely upon the supervisory alliance.

As with psychotherapy, the pedagogical method assumes a secondary position to the interpersonal relationship in our supervision. We invite supervisees to recognize their preoccupation with technique at the expense of the relationship, which Mahoney (1986) labeled the "tyranny of technique." Techniques are most adequately construed as strategies for structuring and communicating the therapeutic message, but they should not be confused with it.

With experienced supervisees, we strive for mutuality in psychotherapy supervision. The ideal relationship can be characterized as a process of mutual exploration and bidirectional exchanges with an "inquiring colleague" (Kagan, 1980). While not abdicating our professional responsibilities nor denying disparities in knowledge and power between us, supervisors strive for an empathic and collaborative relationship. We hope to create an environment that encourages trainees to express their insecurities, to disagree respectfully, and to suggest alternatives—even if these temporarily increase discomfort. A critical question that guides us is, "Will supervisees present what makes them look bad or only what makes them look good?"

In a later chapter of this book, I (LMP) describe sharing with my integrative supervisor (JCN) a section of video-recorded supervision that went poorly. I did not hesitate to do so because our relationship was solid, and I trusted him to guide me through a better outcome minus any judgment. Rarely do we learn from our successes. We learn from the times

we failed and the hope that "I will not do that again." I threw my insecurities to the wayside to build my skills as a therapist. Our supervisory alliance enabled me to do so. I encourage all supervisees to do the same. Supervisors hold in their hands the ability to make or break the spirit of future clinicians through the alliance they create. The supervisory relationship is paramount. Explore the relationship, nurture it, and, if at all possible, enjoy it.

## What Works and What Doesn't

Perhaps the most important research on supervision concerns the relational predispositions and styles of the supervisor. Review after review (e.g., M. V. Ellis, 2010; Neufeldt, Beutler, & Banchero, 1997) echoes the same conclusion: The ideal supervisor possesses "high levels of empathy, respect, genuineness, flexibility, concern, investment, and openness" (Carifio & Hess, 1987, p. 244). Like good therapists, good supervisors use appropriate teaching, goal setting, and feedback. They tend to be seen as supportive, noncritical individuals who respect their supervisees and avoid turning the supervisory experience into psychotherapy. Other supervision styles that lead to a stronger working alliance are the supervisors' ethical integrity, above-average intelligence, and strong listening skills (Bucky, Marques, Daly, Alley, & Karp, 2010).

Supervisor disclosure of his or her therapy experiences has been shown to not only improve the supervisory relationship but also ease the shame and discomfort that supervisees may feel about their own experiences (Farber, 2006). Such self-disclosure allows supervisees to breathe a proverbial sigh of relief and recognize that their supervisor is a fallible human as opposed to a deity. Research shows that self-disclosure leads to a better working alliance and more satisfaction on the part of both the supervisor and the supervisee (Knox, Burkard, Edwards, Smith, & Schlosser, 2008).

One of us (JCN) was impressed in his own training by an early study of objectionable supervisory styles (Rosenblatt & Mayer, 1975). Researchers found four styles to be particularly problematic: constrictive, amorphous,

unsupportive, and therapeutic. It is important for supervisors to remain focused during supervision sessions, be mindful of time constraints, support supervisees liberally, and challenge the supervisee effectively to improve the relationship between supervisor and supervisee.

Supervisees complain bitterly of two more detrimental styles of supervisors: remote and authoritarian (G. J. Allen, Szollos, & Williams, 1986; Moskowitz & Rupert, 1983; M. L. Nelson & Friedlander, 2001). The remote and uncommitted style tends to beget trainee struggle or extensive anger. In such relationships, supervisees commonly lose trust, feel unsafe, pull back, and remain guarded. Supervisors who demand conformity and punish divergence from the "party line" jeopardize their supervisory relationship and subvert central tenets of integration.

One of us (LMP) endured just such a dogmatic, domineering supervisor during doctoral studies. The supervisor's power was used as a tool of retribution for any disagreement or perceived deviation from what the supervisor saw as the true path of therapy. The cumulative effects on me were mistrust of my individual style of clinical work and inhibition of my personality while conducting psychotherapy. For others, it potentially meant dismissal and/or failure of the class. Much like controlling parents produce inhibited children, controlling superiors produce inhibited clinicians and take the "real" part of the clinician out of the experience. The damage can take years to undo.

The grim truth is that not all supervisory relationships prove positive, and a considerable portion of supervisees feel harmed by their supervisor (M. V. Ellis, 2006). A stifled environment for supervisees leads to fear of retribution in the form of grades, written evaluations, and possibly departmental politics. More than one graduate student has attributed a negative supervisory experience to subsequent losses of teaching assistantships, difficulty forming dissertation committees, and unenthusiastic letters of recommendation. Supervisors may have to undo damage that a previous supervisor has done—a reality for which I (JCN) was unprepared in my early years supervising.

Supervisees tend to be most vulnerable to harsh criticism at the beginning of their training when they are less confident in their abilities as therapists (Stoltenberg & Delworth, 1987; Tryon, 1996). If they do not enjoy a good

working relationship with a supervisor during that critical developmental period, they may not feel comfortable as a therapist and their growth may suffer. Indeed, a weak alliance between supervisor and supervisee has been shown to lead supervisees to feel disillusioned with the field. They may question the profession they chose, suffer from high anxiety about meeting with their supervisors, and mistrust the process of supervision (Gray, Ladany, Walker, & Ancis, 2001; M. L. Nelson & Friedlander, 2001).

Relationship factors consistently emerge as the most important determinants of positive outcome in psychotherapy (Norcross & Lambert, 2014), and similar importance can be attributed to relationship factors in supervision—not only in that particular supervisory dyad but in the whole of clinical training. Research suggests the supervisory relationship proves one of the most influential factors in a supervisee's satisfaction with his or her overall training (Ramos-Sánchez et al., 2002).

Article after article in the supervision literature nominates one or another relationship feature as the neglected but essential ingredient. At the risk of contributing to that morass, let us nominate *trust*. Without trust, nothing of significance seems to start and nothing of import seems to eventuate. There is never a single ingredient, of course, but to our minds, trust comes the closest to it in integrative supervision. And trust can happily coexist with challenge and learning.

As should now be evident, the relationship is simultaneously a context and a process for change in supervision. We as integrative supervisors have the opportunity of providing our students with wonderful gifts. Ideally, they will finish their work with us knowing more about therapy, more about clients, more about us, and, most important, more about themselves. They will be enthusiastic about their calling and the effectiveness of systematic integration (Halgin, 1986). The integrative supervisory relationship offers an optimal, in vivo context within which to promote these crucial goals.

## Parallel Process

Parallel processes between supervision and psychotherapy can take many forms, which are sadly not frequently distinguished in the literature. In one manifestation, supervisees may behave in supervision in a similar way

to how their patient behaves in psychotherapy—say, in a self-denigrating or nondisclosing manner. This is occasionally, but not necessarily, the case. In another manifestation of parallel process, the dynamics between supervisee and supervisor may mimic those of the therapeutic relationship. Supervisees bring similar interpersonal and defensive patterns to all relationships. This, we believe, is inevitably the case (Norcross, 1988).

In both of these cases of parallel process, the supervisor can and should address these repetitive relationship patterns. To do so enhances the trainee's awareness and performance in all interpersonal pursuits, including but not limited to conducting psychotherapy. Should supervisee awareness and supervisor attention to any seriously maladaptive patterns not suffice to remediate them, then referral for personal therapy is warranted.

A related but distinct form of parallel process occurs in integrative supervision. We intentionally adapt both to supervisees conducting their psychotherapy and to supervisors conducting their supervision. We are continually involved in a parallel process of tailoring supervision to each of our students as they tailor the psychological treatment to each of their clients. The net result is a synergistic enterprise that fits supervisor, supervisee–therapist, and client with improved outcomes for all.

## EVALUATION

Evaluation in supervision covers four dimensions: evaluating the outcomes of the patients being treated by the supervisee; evaluating the supervisee's performance; evaluating the supervisor him- or herself; and evaluating the supervision (as conceptually distinct from the supervisor). We offer a few words and suggestions on each.

### Evaluation of Patients

In integrative supervision, we strongly urge—some would say "require"— trainees to monitor the progress and evaluate the outcome of the therapy they render. This process occurs formatively (during therapy) and

summatively (posttherapy). In the former, we frequently use one of the dozen or so feedback monitoring systems (see Hilsenroth, 2015). We typically focus on one of three feedback systems: the free Session Rating Scale (SRS V.3.0; Duncan et al., 2003; containing four items evaluating the quality of the relationship, goals and topics, approach or method, and overall satisfaction); Lambert's (2010; http://www.oqmeasures.com) computerized Outcome Questionnaire (containing 30 or 45 items); or the InnerLife STS (Systematic Treatment Selection; http://innerlife.com/), a 100-plus item, cloud-based assessment of patient problem areas, patient transdiagnostic characteristics, and treatment recommendations based on STS principles. On the SRS, the patient rates the relationship for the session, approach or method used during the session, and overall satisfaction with the session on an analog scale, 1 through 10, where the left represents extreme dissatisfaction and the right represents complete satisfaction. The developers of the measure recommend exploration with any score lower than an 8 or 9 (Duncan et al., 2003).

Sometimes supervisees read about and experiment with one of the other feedback methods. If doing so is more aligned with the therapy itself or supervisee preferences, the supervisee will hold an explicit discussion with the client about the quality of their relationship, goal attainment, the approach, what is working, and what can be improved. The important point is to explicitly ask; therapists who specifically and respectfully inquire about their client's perceptions of therapy and the relationship frequently enhance the alliance and prevent premature termination.

Summative evaluation of patients occurs generally as the particular therapy approach or supervisee recommends, but occur it does, in the form of serial administration of symptom measures, collateral reports, broad measures of psychopathology, positive well-being instruments, goal attainment scales, relationship functioning, and so on. In our supervisory relationship, LMP opted to use serial assessment of the Counseling Center Assessment of Psychological Symptoms (CCAPS; Youn et al., 2015) as a primary determinant of treatment outcome because her college center routinely administered it at the initiation of services.

Another primary determinant of summative outcome entails a candid exchange with patients, which feels natural because these discussions have regularly happened by means of formative evaluation throughout the course of therapy. I (JCN) ask supervisees to routinely ask clients and themselves at the end of treatment several questions: What proved most effective in therapy? What seemed to work? What is left to work on? How could I have been even more effective? Supervisees quickly learn the centrality of the relationship for clients, even when the therapy feels technique-oriented to the supervisee.

## Evaluation of Supervisees

For evaluating supervisee competence in particular systems of psychotherapy, we incorporate formal methods that have evolved from treatment manuals. Criteria-based rating scales for assessing technical skill have been developed for numerous psychotherapies, and these scales are profitably applied to the audio and video recordings on which our integrative supervision is based. By the same token, ratings of relationship competencies can be adapted from training materials and manuals.

Becoming proficient in relational and technical skills will prove of little value if the supervisee has not learned when and with whom to use them. Our supervision thus adds another facet of supervisee evaluation: treatment planning for integrative work. Competence in integrative case formulation, selected assessments, and the recognition of client markers for applying different methods—we look for these abilities in video-recorded sessions, of course, but also within supervision sessions, case presentations, work samples, simulated interviews, and adherence to integrative manuals.

For evaluating broader supervisee skills, we rate performance on structured lists of professional competencies. For psychologists, the competency benchmarks (Fouad et al., 2009; see also http://www.apa.org/ed/graduate/benchmarks-evaluation-system.aspx) provide multiple competencies across training level (e.g., first practicum, readiness for independent practice). As part of the written contract, the supervisee and supervisor

determine early which broad competencies will be targeted and serve as goals; not all of the professional competencies, such as teaching or conducting research, will be the object of every supervision.

The American Psychological Association (APA) benchmarks represent broad professional competencies. The categories consist of professionalism, reflective practice/self-assessment, self-care, scientific knowledge and methods, relationships, individual and cultural diversity, ethical and legal standards, interdisciplinary systems, assessment, intervention, consultation, research/evaluation, teaching, management/administration, and advocacy. Within each category are several particular items to be rated, each on a scale of unsatisfactory, satisfactory, good, and excellent.

Frequency of summative evaluation depends upon the supervisory context and trainee need. For psychology interns or residents seeking licensure in Pennsylvania, for instance, formal written evaluations must occur at least quarterly. For psychology doctoral students, we complete formal evaluations at the end of each semester using the APA competency benchmarks. For licensed practitioners undergoing integrative supervision with me (JCN), written summative evaluations typically do not occur. Instead, I rely on frequent formative feedback because formal paperwork is not required.

Following the initial summative evaluation, we typically ask supervisees to rate themselves on the criteria before and independent of our own ratings. This method facilitates supervisee self-reflection, generates a more reciprocal exchange, and explicates the convergence, and any divergences, in our respective perceptions.

## Evaluation of Supervisors

Most advanced practitioners report at least one unsatisfactory experience as supervisees—one in which the theory, the technique, or the style of supervision was discordant with their needs. Most supervisors have experienced a similar uncomfortable experience when something seemed quite wrong with the supervision, yet no solution was immediately apparent. We are convinced that such discordant supervision relationships

suffer from (a) inadequate explication of supervision expectations and goals at the outset (discussed earlier in this chapter) and (b) insufficient evaluation of the supervision throughout.

Over the years I (JCN) have employed a panoply of methods for having supervisees pragmatically evaluate my supervision. To focus the process for supervisees and to reduce their anxiety, I employed structured ratings, written forms, and, for about a decade, the Supervisory Working Alliance Inventory (Horvath & Greenberg, 1989). Having specific content and behavioral anchors helps launch as-candid-as-possible discussion of students' feelings about the supervision. In reality, the supervisor's powerful position makes it difficult for all but the boldest supervisees to share candid feedback with the supervisor. The power differential and student anxiety are potent forces operating against frank evaluations.

In our supervision, we chose the Leeds Alliance in Supervision Scale (LASS; Wainwright, 2010), which parallels the SRS used to evaluate therapy sessions. Every fifth supervision session or so, LMP completed the three-item LASS: rating the supervisor's approach (from *supervision was not focused* to *supervision was focused*), the relationship (from *did not understand each other* to *understood each other*), and meeting my needs (*supervisor not helpful to me* to *supervisor was helpful to me*). That was followed by an open conversation about what is working, what is valued, and what can be improved.

Following his review of supervision research, Worthington (1987) concluded that, unlike clinicians who frequently improve with experience, supervisors do not necessarily become better supervisors over time. Worthington speculated that this may be attributable to the minimal attention devoted in professional environments to the advancement of supervision. We speculate that an additional reason lies in the dearth of evaluation of supervisors and supervision. Increasing supervision skill requires constant feedback from others and a desire to improve.

As a supervisee, I (LMP) strongly suggest offering honest feedback to your supervisor, presuming a strong alliance. As a therapist, I have found that receiving less than stellar feedback in supervision has catapulted a stagnant process into a more meaningful experience and tremendous

growth. Good supervisors desire to adapt supervision to your unique needs, so they need your input to do so. In a good-enough supervisory relationship, the data are always friendly.

### Evaluation of Supervision

It may prove difficult to conceptually distinguish between the supervisor and the supervision as a whole, but we do recommend that supervision dyads take a few moments periodically to take a higher, bird's-eye view of the supervision and the training content in which it transpires. Such a perspective can help diffuse any strong negative feelings toward each other and readdress the supervision objectives. Is the supervision itself assisting the trainee to achieve good client outcomes? Apart from any positive or negative feelings toward the particular supervisor (or supervisee), is this supervision building competencies? Is the supervision, enjoyable or not, protecting the public from incompetent or ineffective services?

Research has consistently determined that most clinical training programs have not systematically evaluated their impact on trainees, nor their trainees' impact on clients. If we are serious about enhancing the development of psychotherapists, then such evaluations are crucial. Where are the gaps, locally and nationally, in the supervision enterprise?

## FEEDBACK

Integrative supervisors provide feedback to students in a variety of ways within a coherent framework. Of course, at first feedback may be uncomfortable for the supervisor to provide and the supervisee to receive, but after continued use it all becomes easier, even routine. Ideally, feedback in supervision occurs seamlessly over time, within a warm relationship, and in a bidirectional fashion. Useful feedback strengthens the supervisory relationship and client outcomes. We construe feedback as expected, natural, and safe. The supervisor requesting and welcoming supervisee feedback creates a safer place for improvement by all concerned.

The following transcript provides an example from one of our supervision sessions in which supervisee feedback is expected and given. The

supervisor anticipates and articulates that, out of anxiety and a need to please, the supervisee might rate him higher than she might actually feel. We recommend such explicit communication in supervision, which parallels that done with clients in their feedback about their therapy satisfaction. We structure the expectations to receive as candid and as accurate feedback as possible.

Supervisors and supervisees frequently develop a shared shorthand of verbal communication, as frequently do therapists and clients. Thus, we have annotated and explained below several of our shorthand expressions.

Toward the end of the supervision session, the supervisor (JCN) recognizes that they are approaching the end of the scheduled time and transitions to another topic with the supervisee (LMP):

**JCN:** Another delicious moment in parallel processing. . . . So, I'm being mindful of the time; anything else urgent?

**LMP:** No.

**JCN:** Well, it is our 30th session, and I'm encouraging you to give these feedback measures (to clients). (Supervisor directs attention to the feedback form.) This will be, I think, your fifth one.

**LMP:** Yes.

**JCN:** Yes. And the pressure? ("Pressure" refers to social and evaluative pressure to rate the supervisor favorably.)

**LMP:** Low.

**JCN:** Low? 4ish?

**LMP:** 3 . . . 4.

**JCN:** Oh. If I keep asking you, will it keep getting lower?

**LMP:** (Chuckling)

**JCN:** Great, so let's talk.

**LMP:** OK.

**JCN:** Please, your honest impression so we can go forward.

**LMP:** OK. (She completes the three-item supervision feedback measure. They are all high. The approach works.)

**JCN:** (Reviewing the supervisee's ratings) So the supervision approach was focused?

**LMP:** Yes.

**JCN:** You felt understood....

**LMP:** Yes.

**JCN:** And it was helpful.

**LMP:** Absolutely. The reading (discussed during supervision) will be doubly helpful.

**JCN:** Oh, let me give that to you before I forget. You know how I can be (referring to supervisor's penchant for discussing a reading during the session but forgetting to deliver it to the supervisee at the end of their session).

**LMP:** Thank you (supervisee takes the article offered by the supervisor).

**JCN:** So that is Steven Finn, and on the back are some references too. When you read it, you are going to find some real convergence to what you've done. He (Finn) would have probably said talk a little more about the purpose of the assessment.

**LMP:** OK.

**JCN:** And then perhaps a summary at the end (of the therapy session) or a written summary. Perhaps that won't prove necessary in your relationship. I think you'll be surprised; you intuitively did lots of things that are recommended in the research. (The topic concerns providing therapeutic feedback from the results of psychological testing; see http://www.therapeutic assessment.com/about.html.)

**LMP:** OK.

**JCN:** Well (returning to the feedback ratings), I do feel that things are going well in our relationship and we're following very nicely with each other. But we can always do a little better, yes?

**LMP:** OK.

**JCN:** So, without being perfectionist, what would you have on your mind? How can we make the good even better?

**LMP:** I think more constructive feedback maybe, and I enjoy the readings so anytime there is something I can read when I am struggling a little bit with anything in therapy is helpful so. . . .

**JCN:** Can I borrow the pen?

**LMP:** Sure.

**JCN:** I will make a note for next time so we follow up on the collaborative therapeutic assessment.

**LMP:** OK. Yes, it's helpful to talk about it. Also any of the readings you assign.

**JCN:** And do you have someone else (a client) coming up? For example, a new client that has taken the CCAPS we could go over?

**LMP:** Yes. I have new clients all the time and that is something they have to take . . . and unless something (a test score) is spiked, you know usually like suicidal ideation, I really don't tell them about their scores on the CCAPS. We usually go right into the intake (form).

**JCN:** And now you are thinking you might . . . ?

**LMP:** Now I'm thinking it is probably something I should do.

**JCN:** The good news (of clients' test results), what they didn't score on and perhaps focal areas.

**LMP:** Right.

**JCN:** The collaborative therapeutic assessment model does that as well. Of course, the scores, the overall patterns are important, but so too the idiosyncratic responses—"What were you thinking of when you said occasionally you hear strange noises that other people don't?" At least for me, it puts my mind to rest when they (clients) say, "Yeah, my hearing is good and my bedroom is on the top floor." So I can put to rest that there is not some psychotic process going on.

**LMP:** Right.

**JCN:** So, the collaborative therapeutic assessment, the reading, as well as looking at one or two critical items that you should review on the CCAPS.

**LMP:** Right.

**JCN:** Anything else (returning to what we could improve upon in future supervision sessions)? We don't need to be perfectionistic, but I do want to track what's occurring here.

**LMP:** No, I think we're OK. I think that your feedback is relative and poignant and it definitely helps.

**JCN:** I'm delighted to hear it.

**LMP:** And I appreciate the positives even when I'm feeling very negative.

**JCN:** Have I been at all successful at helping you in moving this (supervisee's negative evaluation of her skill) a little bit?

**LMP:** A little bit, absolutely.

**JCN:** Well, that's enough efficacy for me.

The supervisor intentionally enacts a form of parallel process or modeling: Raise the prospect of, even playfully assess, the pressure for favorable evaluation ratings. That pressure or desire naturally occurs when supervisees evaluate supervisors and when clients evaluate psychotherapy. The point is to encourage honesty and thus obtain more useful, authentic feedback.

As well, the supervisor models—only partly consciously this time—that incremental changes are desirable and acceptable. That occurs in assisting LMP to gradually move her evaluation of her skill in reviewing test results with clients from "very negative" to more realistically neutral. Small changes prove "enough" and indeed are the rule in life.

Opportunities for self-reflection and improvement abound in every therapy session and in every supervision session. Even now, reviewing the transcript, we discern potential enhancements. LMP relearns that she says "OK" too often; JCN finds himself starting sentences with "so" too often

and moves his hands as if, in the words of an observant colleague, he is hatching a plan. Although we understood the transitions and each other throughout, perhaps the switches between the feedback process and the content of the readings were not clear. It is probably better in some cases to handle the process of feedback separately—and sequentially—from a discussion of content and readings. In any event, feedback as a part of learning should be expected, natural, and safe.

Notice in the above exchange that, although the supervision feedback scores were quite positive, the supervisor pushed the supervisee to express areas in which improvements could be achieved. This insistence on the "good getting better" helps put the supervisee at ease and yet opens the door to express what needs may not be met. One of the top requests from supervisees is for the supervisor to stay focused on what is relevant to them and their clients (Bucky et al., 2010). Using regular feedback in supervision is a prime way to ensure that the supervisees' needs are being met and the supervisor stays on task.

Some supervisors and most supervisees will feel uncomfortable with this direct feedback process at first. Supervisors may not want to hear what supervisees have to say, and supervisees may be hesitant to say anything negative to their supervisor. Rest assured, with time, practice, and goodwill, feedback becomes a normal part of the experience and enhances supervision. In the preceding exchange, the supervisor jokingly inquiries whether, if he keeps asking the supervisee how tempted she feels to rate him favorably, that pressure will continue to decrease until there is no pressure at all. The truth is there will always be some desire to placate the supervisor, but within a trusted relationship that desire will be eclipsed by the desire to learn and assist clients to succeed.

## THE CONTEXT/SETTING

Integrative supervision is relevant to and conducted in all practice settings. The context may be hospital units, day programs, outpatient clinics, counseling centers, or independent practices. Ages and diagnoses of the clientele are similarly broad and varied. I (JCN) have provided integrative

supervision physically in all of those contexts and to practitioners working in all of them.

Interestingly, inpatient units and brief outpatient settings proved most congenial to integration in its development. The brief, problem focus of the two settings brought formerly different therapies closer together and created variations of psychological treatments that are more compatible with each other. Integration responds to the pragmatic time-limited injunction of "whatever therapy works better—and quicker—for this particular patient." In an early study of 294 HMO therapists, for instance, the prevalence of integration as a theoretical orientation nearly doubled as a function of their employment in HMOs favoring brief psychotherapy (Austad, Sherman, Morgan, & Holstein, 1992).

Many practitioners gravitate to integration as they acquire clinical experience, like LMP, and when they treat difficult patients who do not respond favorably or completely to pure-form monotherapies. People with personality disorders, eating disorders, substance abuse, posttraumatic stress disorder, obsessive–compulsive disorder, and chronic mental illnesses, to name a few, are among such difficult patients. Integrative treatments and supervisors tend to predominate in these settings, with greater emphasis on the clinical problem than on their theoretical orientation per se.

A challenge for (and a fascination of) clinical supervisors is to adapt supervision to the environmental context in which services are offered. It makes little sense to supervise long-term therapy in a college counseling center that provides a maximum of 14 sessions, for example. Practitioners, and supervisors, learn to adapt quickly. All good supervisors tailor supervision to the particular setting, but integrative supervisors arguably prove more fluid, systematic, and experienced in doing so.

# 3

# Supervisory Methods

Integrative supervision is necessarily eclectic in therapeutic content and pedagogical method. In terms of content, the supervisor's work is determined by both the needs of the clients being discussed and the needs of the trainee. Thus, one supervision or one supervision session might entail a directive/educative approach in which the trainee learns specific techniques for the treatment of a focused clinical problem. Another supervision or another session with the same supervisee might involve an approach that is predominantly exploratory, because of either the historical roots of the client's conflicts or the countertransference struggles of the therapist (Halgin & Murphy, 1995).

Methodologically, integrative supervision entails a wide variety of techniques and stances associated with diverse psychotherapy systems. Structure should follow function. As the situation dictates, supervision might involve didactic presentations, reading assignments, open-ended

discussions, personal modeling, experiential activities, video review, case examples, and mini case conferences. Supervisors may need to adapt interpersonal stances across supervisees and even in their work with each supervisee when their clients are treated with divergent interventions.

Supervision of integrative clinical work should be, as we have argued, tailored to the particular needs of the supervisee and the dictates of the situation. We remain skeptical about universal recommendations based on select trainees and limited contexts. The determinants of behavior are too numerous and supervisees' needs too heterogeneous to provide the identical supervisory experience to each and every student.

In this chapter, we try to put meat onto the skeleton of the integrative supervision we have outlined thus far. We address the methods of integrative supervision: creating its rationale, selecting the methods, providing documentation, adapting supervision to the individual trainee and context, and deciding on the mix of supervision formats.

## CREATING A RATIONALE

The rationale for integrative supervision is compelling: Humans differ, and when any complex human enterprise—supervision, psychotherapy, learning, relationships—is systematically adapted to those individual and cultural differences, then humans prosper. One size, one theory, one method does not fit all. In dramatic moments, I (JCN) have been known to exclaim, "Let us be the responsive and effective ones!" Trainees immediately seize upon this frame, and research consistently supports its effectiveness.

### A Needs Assessment

Supervisees invariably present with multiple agendas, some manifest and some latent, and diverse needs, some of which are quite out of their awareness. As in clinical work, supervision can ideally begin with a needs assessment: What do supervisees want and/or need from the supervisory experience? Are they here to facilitate personal growth? To ventilate about therapy frustrations? To validate their theoretical allegiances? To evaluate technical weaknesses? To analyze countertransferential reactions? To

achieve all of these (e.g., "to become a better therapist") or none of these (e.g., "because I was assigned to you")? Initial and continual redefinition of supervision objectives is required.

Of course, the supervisee's preferences will conflict on occasion with the supervisor's judgment as to legitimate needs. For example, when I asked how he best handled negative feedback in supervision, one advanced trainee seriously replied, "By ignoring it"! However, as in this case, the disparities sometimes are uncovered early by tactful inquiry and can become a focus of supervision. The supervisee's desires should be elicited, articulated, and considered but will not necessarily commit the supervisor to that tack (Norcross, Beutler, & Clarkin, 1990).

## A Systematic Model

A systematic model determines in large part whether integrative supervision is experienced as intelligible or bewildering. Supervision within a coherent framework is associated with a higher quality experience (D. M. Allen, Kennedy, Veeser, & Grosso, 2000); conversely, less valued integrative supervisors fail to ground their clinical interventions within larger conceptual perspectives. These unsystematic integrative supervisors may lack the big picture—an encompassing, integrative structure that organizes the case formulation and prioritizes the clinical intervention. In other words, be integrative, not syncretic.

In the midst of conducting psychotherapy, many supervisees will desire immediate and concrete guidance on the "right" treatment for their patients. In the midst of conducting supervision, a supervisor will want to address the student's immediate need but also provide a more general treatment selection heuristic for future patients. According to directors of doctoral programs, the most frequent integrative models used in this regard appear to be multimodal therapy, the common factors approach, the transtheoretical (stages of change) model, cognitive–interpersonal therapy, and systematic treatment selection (Lampropoulos & Dixon, 2007). Our integrative amalgam borrows heavily from systematic treatment selection, stages of change, multimodal, and common factors; in fact, I (JCN) have collaborated and published with the founders of each of these

integrative models. Our inescapable point is that supervisors need to offer systematic and evidence-based models.

These integrative models specify the basis for treatment selection and guide the supervisor in enabling supervisees to determine the treatments and relationships of choice. Decisional models are provided for selecting the technical procedures and relationship stances from various therapeutic orientations to be applied in given circumstances and with given clients. All told, integrative models provide the coherence and guidance by which a multiplicity of theories and methods can be organized into an integrated understanding. We return to the details of doing so in a subsequent section on adapting supervision.

### *Both/And* Frame

The integrative frame embraces *both/and* instead of *either/or*. The culture wars of psychotherapy have pitted the therapy relationship against the treatment method or the idiographic against the nomothetic. It is easy for trainees to choose sides, ignore disconfirming research, and lose sight of the superordinate commitment to patient benefit. The incontrovertible but oft-neglected truth about psychotherapy is that it is, at once, a relationship and a method. In integrative supervision, we focus on crafting the best of each for the supervisee and for the supervisee to craft the best relationship stance and technical methods for each client. Similarly, we aim to blend the idiographic and the nomothetic, the particular and the general. One means of doing so is to adapt psychotherapy to the particulars of the individual patient according to generalities identified by research. Many specious dualities, thankfully, fade away in integrative supervision. The clinical phenomena become fuller, richer, more verdant—and more consequential for those receiving our services.

## SELECTING SUPERVISION METHODS

The selection of supervision methods is driven largely by (a) the goals and methods of the psychotherapy case under consideration, (b) their responsive fit with the supervisee, and, when available, (c) the results of empirical

research as to their relative efficacy. It is crucial to have a clear sense of the goals of the psychotherapy case, which can then inform the methods of supervision (Goldberg, 1985; Tennen, 1988). Supervision goals range from teaching a supervisee technical aspects of a client–therapist interaction to focusing on the affective associations of the therapist to the client. In the former, assigning the supervisee readings on the technique, watching an expert demonstrating it on video, and practicing it in the supervision might prove to be the methods of choice. In the latter, asking the supervisee to take extensive process notes and articulate emotional reactions as he or she watches the video or reviews the process note proves more concordant with the goal. Goals of supervision usually reflect goals of therapy, and the goals of therapy are typically rooted in a theoretical perspective.

Within limits of feasibility and creativity, the *how* of supervision (method) should be consistent with the *what* of supervision (content). In other words, the supervision approach mirrors the therapeutic approach (Frances & Clarkin, 1981). When the supervisee's treatment approach entails verbal, insight-oriented work, supervision may profitably explore the student's countertransference reactions to both client and supervisor. Similarly, didactic instruction and role playing in the supervision hour are especially congruent with more behavioral, action-oriented approaches.

At the same time, we find value in conceptualizing supervision as a complement to treatment. Work on countertransference, for example, is not limited to the supervision of insight-oriented treatment but also extends to students who are prone to ignore it in treatment (Stricker, 1988). (The second and third drivers of the choice of supervision methods are covered in subsequent sections of this book.)

Over the decades, I (JCN) have utilized and experimented with a number of supervision methods. These include, inter alia, live observation, cotherapy (with beginning supervisees), review of audio recordings and now video recordings, process notes, case summaries, and discussion of a session's critical incidents. Each method has its relative advantages and disadvantages, and the supervision dyad performs an informal cost–benefit analysis of these supervisory techniques.

Cotherapy tends to undermine the power and confidence of the beginning therapist as well as complicate the real and transferential relationship.

I frown on the method except as necessary with beginning therapists. Case summaries and reviews of critical incidents are useful at times but frequently obscure the larger therapeutic process. In the past, I was a fan of process notes for their informational and relational richness, but they often lack objectivity.

Observation behind a one-way mirror is desirable and arranged whenever mutual schedules permit. Live supervision may or may not be involved as part of that real-time observation, depending again on the trainee's competence and needs. Video recording seems less intrusive and distracting than live observation.

Importantly, we have moved away from reliance on supervisees' self-reports and "reconstructed tales of therapy" (Norcross, 1988) to the use of video and live observation through one-way mirrors. This progression has substantially increased the accuracy and completeness of information about what has ensued in therapy and thereby has enhanced supervision. Despite its intrusive nature, video recording provides the best compromise and has achieved a consensus as the best method for conducting supervision. The empirical research tends to support review of video-recorded therapy sessions, supervision guidelines encourage it, and several jurisdictions (e.g., Pennsylvania, American Psychological Association accreditation) now mandate a minimum number of observations (video-recorded or live) of supervisees' performance. Supervisees' evaluations (G. J. Allen, Szollos, & Williams, 1986; G. Nelson, 1978) and empirical research (e.g., M. V. Ellis, 2010) indicate that direct observation and videos are the preferred supervisory methods. Although supervisees find it difficult to watch themselves on tape, video offers both the supervisee and the supervisor an opportunity to discern patterns and catch behaviors of which the supervisee was unaware.

## Watching Tape

In the following transcript from a discussion that appears in the DVD *Integrative Psychotherapy Supervision*, the supervisor (JCN) and supervisee

(LMP) are discussing with the cohost of the series, Hanna Levenson (HL), the integral role that video-recording sessions play in integrative supervision.

**HL:** What was it like videotaping your sessions?

**LMP:** The sessions aren't bad to videotape. You get used to the camera in session pretty quickly and ignore that it's there. It's watching the videotapes after that.... (JCN and HL chuckling) It's never comfortable. Even now, I have been doing it for how long and I am still uncomfortable. I think that speaks to the relationship with the supervisor (JCN) that I can show things that I am uncomfortable with or not proud of. I knew ahead of time that this (session) did not go well, and I still wanted to show it. I think video is so important. There are times when I will think things went really well, and he (JCN) will pick things out about what I missed where I would not have seen had I not videotaped. I know it is part of the growth process.

**HL:** Thank you. And John, how much is use of video an integral part of this approach?

**JCN:** It is central. We really do need to see what is occurring.... I also might add that it never gets easy watching the videotape. For example, sometimes I notice that I overuse words like "so" and "right." Sometimes I don't know what I'm doing with my hands. (Simulates a mad scientist hatching a scheme with hands) I don't know if I am knitting or creating clay....

In a video-recorded therapy session, LMP's client was visibly upset about the results of the psychological test, but the supervisee did not see it because she was looking down while reading the results of the test. The client agreed whenever the supervisee looked up from the test. If not for the video, LMP would have probably come to supervision saying that the feedback of the Millon test went surprisingly well because the client agreed the whole time.

And this is what I (LMP) thought until I saw the video during supervision. The client was rolling her eyes and shaking her head when hearing certain test results. I did not have the best session because I was neither skilled nor experienced in giving test feedback; it felt like I was disjointed.

However, I had no idea there was so much nonverbal pushback from the client until we watched the video. Although this example is extreme (rarely do video recordings of therapy show clients making faces at their therapists), video reviews do afford a second look at what transpires in a session. You can bet the next time I share testing results with my clients I will be looking straight at them and asking them to express their true reactions.

When watching video, we request the supervisee's input throughout. Where did you feel stuck? Where did things soar? What is another way of looking at that? How did that new perspective or skill work out? The supervisor invites the trainee's impressions before commenting, a sequence that enhances the skill of supervisee self-reflection and tempers supervisor judgmentalism. We regularly probe perfectionistic trainees to identify the strengths of the observed transaction to counter their immediate and sometimes overwhelming "what went wrong" answers.

For decades, failed experiences have been considered the most powerful sources of learning, but recent research demonstrates that, through systematic reflection, supervisees learn from both their successes and failures (S. Ellis, Carette, Anseel, & Lievens, 2014). Three functions characterize systematic reflection: self-explanation (supervisees are asked to analyze their own behavior and advance suggestions), data verification (supervisees are challenged with different perceptions of the same data, which enables them to sidestep biases), and feedback (performance evaluation and focus on helping supervisees systematically analyze their decisions that produced those performance outcomes). The three steps sound cumbersome, but they occur naturally and sequentially in prompting self-reflection:

1. What happened and what might account for that? Or, what led you to do A rather than B?
2. What might have happened with a different approach?
3. What worked, and what did not? We try to prompt and model supervisees through the steps.

Supervisees can learn from both successful and unsuccessful experiences through reflection, but the focus of the reflection shifts. After a failed

experience, the biggest performance improvement typically occurs when the supervisory dyad focuses on both correct and erroneous performances. However, after a successful experience, the biggest performance improvement often occurs when the dyad reflects on the erroneous actions only. That's a valuable lesson from psychological science (S. Ellis et al., 2014): Learning is most likely to ensue from disciplined reflection on what could have gone wrong within a trusting, open, and conscientious relationship.

In addition, we highly recommend that supervisees prepare a verbatim transcript of one or two entire sessions. This task can become an odious time suck, especially if the supervisee is not a fluid typist, but supervisors and supervisees have found the process instructive. Transcripts or intense observation of video segments permit microanalysis of critical exchanges. That sort of analysis promotes more experiential learning (as contrasted with cognitive learning) and more implicit learning. In fact, most intense microanalyses in integrative supervision immediately give way to supervisees' countertransferential material and efforts to learn improved case formulation or therapy skills.

For instance, I (LMP) discovered many times I would ask my client open-ended questions and not allow the client enough time to answer. My own anxiety and "helping" efforts were impeding the therapeutic work. In reviewing a session transcript, I found that after some hesitation by the client I would jump in and offer the client a number of options from which to choose. JCN pointed out that I was working hard to make it easy for my client. I found this to be a recurrent pattern and became aware of it in ongoing sessions with many clients.

The client whose session I (LMP) transcribed was one in which I had a hard time getting a word in edgewise. She would take a deep breath and talk nonstop without room for me to interject. However, upon transcribing the session I found, in fact, she did allow me multiple opportunities to enter the dialogue. I was not taking them. Be forewarned of the time warp that ensues in transcribing a 50-minute session; nonetheless, doing so gave me valuable insight into my clinical interaction and style. Those included words that I tend to overuse (such as "OK" and "uh huh") and other areas for improvement.

## Integrative Methods

Our preceding recommendations represent a consensus of sorts across theoretical orientations; now we offer several distinctive integrative methods for conducting supervision. We have found the following effective in expanding our own theoretical horizons, and naturally we occasionally try them in supervision:

- We formulate the case under consideration in supervision from disparate theoretical perspectives, leading students to examine points of convergence and contention (Saltzman & Norcross, 1990), therapeutic choices in the treatment, and relative indications and contraindications for particular treatments.
- We try a more sophisticated approach that involves formulating the same case from multiple integrative perspectives—common factors, transtheoretical model, multimodal therapy, systematic treatment selection—to determine points of convergence and contention among their treatment recommendations.
- When supervision feels staid or stifled, we engage in a series of "thought experiments" for psychotherapists (e.g., Shapiro, 1986) to lift our theoretical blinders and to liberate our restricted thinking. For example, you no longer believe in the efficacy of your therapeutic approach, but your practice remains as successful as ever; payment for therapy is abolished; or your new referral is Albert Einstein.
- We rate video-recorded therapy sessions with standardized forms of different manualized therapies. How does this session rate on the adherence forms of, say, dialectical behavior therapy and transference-focused psychotherapy?
- We occasionally conduct cosupervision with an invited colleague. This approach is particularly beneficial when the treatment involves a specialty with which the primary supervisor is less familiar. For example, a specialized cognitive therapy technique for treating a specific disorder might be more effectively taught by an expert.
- Sometimes a consultant can help a supervision that feels stuck. Borrowed from the systemic tradition, the ideas of a dispassionate consultant

can bring a refreshing view to a case that has stagnated, and therefore become frustrating, for the supervisor and the supervisee. Of course, it takes a modicum of courage for a supervisor to make the public admission that he or she is not omniscient.

- When supervisees become unduly preoccupied with either techniques at the expense of the therapeutic relationship or the relationship to the exclusion of efficacious techniques, I ask them to consider how people change in psychotherapy. They quickly recognize that the *either/or* frame does not serve the best interests of themselves or their clients. Supervisees (and sometimes we as supervisors) recenter into a *both/and* frame.
- Our definition of integrative work in this book emphasizes the synthesis of diverse models of psychotherapy, but as foreshadowed in the early chapters, we also address the synergy of psychotherapy with other healing resources, such as self-help. In that integrative meaning, we devote time in supervision to the probability that the patient may be assisted by self-help resources for a particular problem or life challenge. This broader perspective enlarges the scope of supervision and frequently results in asking the patient if he or she may be interested in a self-help book, autobiography, movie, group, or app (Norcross, Campbell, et al., 2013).

## MODELING AND INSTRUCTING

### Modeling

Although modeling has been shown to be an effective procedure for teaching complex behaviors, it is used surprisingly little in supervising psychotherapy. A rather remarkable situation, when one reflects on it: Can one imagine surgeons, musicians, or teachers not observing the very skills they are expected to acquire? Most educators use consultant techniques to pass on knowledge about the methods of psychotherapy.

We and others (e.g., Lampropoulos, 2003; Norcross & Beutler, 2000) have emphasized the enormous value of demonstrating and modeling psychotherapy to trainees. Trainees fruitfully observe the work of clinical supervisors and watch video-recorded segments of expert clinicians.

Supervisors can ensure that therapists-in-training spend many hours behind the one-way mirror and the video-recording device, not just passively watching, but participating in interactive coding, responding, and anticipating the next move (Vaillant, 1997).

Sharing our clinical work with students initiates a magnificent dialogue in which the supervisor becomes vulnerable. Such vulnerability tends to beget a more trusting, mutual, and open relationship. Supervision can focus on the difficulties encountered by the therapist/supervisor, and the student can develop a greater appreciation of what transpires within the integrative therapy session.

Rather than discuss the mistakes they have committed, most supervisors in our experience are inclined to report the successes they have achieved, thus communicating an inflated sense of competence and self-assurance. By contrast, we prefer to disclose the anxieties and mistakes with which we contend in clinical work. Sometimes I (JCN) speak openly of the dumb-ass comment or missed reflection that characterized a recent session. We all struggle.

In integrative supervision, then, the importance of modeling informed pluralism and synthetic thinking cannot be overemphasized. Not unlike our children, our students learn to emulate what we do more closely than what we say (Beutler et al., 1987). But too often, supervisors teach integration in the form of value *statements* instead of value *actions*. Supervisors should reliably model the curiosity and incisiveness central to psychotherapy success as well as to psychotherapy integration.

The following excerpt comes from a supervision session in which the integrative supervisor (JCN) models and the supervisee (LMP) shares emotional reactions.

**JCN:** You have some clients terminating, and I am mindful that it is something you wanted to talk about. You know, that's a real paradox in supervision and therapy. We almost always watch the intake but not so much the good-bye.

**LMP:** Yes; and these are my first clients that I have seen for all 4 years as freshmen, sophomores, juniors, and now they are leaving as seniors. So

these are really, I don't want to say, my first terminations because they are not, but my first long-term clients that I am terminating with.

**JCN:** It's a big deal.

**LMP:** It is.

**JCN:** You're graduating right along with them.

**LMP:** I am.

**JCN:** Given your interest in reading material, there is a delightful quick summary and checklist on termination by Rebecca Curtis from Adelphi (University). I have the PDF and will send it to you.

**LMP:** That would be great.

**JCN:** And I would love to see some of that video. It's going to be emotional.

**LMP:** It is.

**JCN:** And you are tracking your—I hate to call it countertransference—your emotional reaction. This is the time you're graduating.... Is it going to be difficult for you?

**LMP:** Yes (nodding in agreement).

**JCN:** All right.

Here, the supervisor invites the supervisee to bring her emotional reaction into the session. The integrative model welcomes the emotional part and reactivity of the session. In integrative supervision, nothing is out of bounds. Certainly not distinctive to integrative work, the therapist's emotional reactions profoundly influence the treatment outcomes and relationships.

This exchange in a supervision session strikes us as consequential in terms of process and content. The content concerns termination, obviously a major part of the therapeutic enterprise. The emotional loss after long-term treatment is ubiquitous. The supervisee had not previously discussed her impending feelings of loss because she had not previously seen patients over a course of 4 years.

The process of the supervisee acknowledging and confiding her loss is enabled by a trusting relationship, a willing supervisee, and prior modeling and encouragement of sharing emotional reactions in supervision. It would feel odd and abrupt to ignore the emotions surrounding termination. The supervisory process liberated the supervisee to subsequently share her loss with clients in session. In fact, the supervisee as a beginning therapist rarely discussed her feelings or invited clients to discuss their feelings about termination.

This aspect of integrative supervision proved new and different for me (LMP). I never realized in previous training that I could have, and should have, discussed my feelings of terminating with clients. How unfortunate for my clients, who probably felt as if they were on a conveyor belt of treatment and simply fell off the end when it came their time. By sharing my feelings with clients, I am being genuine not only to me but also with them. I am modeling appropriate reactions and skilled goodbyes with clients. It was refreshing to have a place in supervision to process those feelings and to have them encouraged and normalized. If I (LMP) recall correctly, the supervisor (JCN) confided that he had frequently been tearful in saying goodbye to his long-term patients. It is a lesson I will carry with me throughout my own career as a supervisor.

## Instruction

Much has already been said about instruction during integrative supervision—readings between sessions, watching experts perform, practicing new skills, and the like. We characterize the supervision session as a safe place to learn, practice, and, at times, struggle. Perhaps the supervisee skirmishes with how to phrase a process comment, how to interrupt gracefully, how to accelerate the emotional process. Multiple methods are bounced around, one or two chosen and then rehearsed as time permits. Perhaps the supervisee is unaware of strong transferential or countertransferential emotions expressed in session. The supervisor shares what he or she observed, explores their potential sources within the supervisee, and then instructs on researched methods for managing countertransference

(Hayes, Gelso, & Hummel, 2011). Or perhaps the supervisee is not knowledgeable or skilled in a particular treatment method indicated for a particular patient or moment. We might jump to a quick tutorial (with readings and video between supervision sessions) on, for instance, motivational interviewing for a precontemplator, empty chair for processing unfinished business, or a couples communication exercise for underskilled partners. All are the stuff of instruction and coaching in supervision.

As mentioned previously, supervisees may also benefit by learning how seasoned therapists themselves struggled in their attempts to develop an integrated approach. This can occur by sharing the supervisor's own trajectory or by reading about other integrative therapists (Goldfried, 2001).

A recent article, subtitled "How responsive supervisors train responsive psychotherapists" (Friedlander, 2015), beautifully captures the relational context in which instruction occurs within supervision. Friedlander articulated several practical relational strategies to help trainees repair alliance ruptures, those tensions and breaks in the therapy relationship. She convincingly demonstrated that modeling, supervisory alliance, responsiveness, and instruction seamlessly flow in promoting supervisee growth. Although possible to separate modeling and instruction and the relationship as conceptual categories, as done here, our experience in supervision holds that they are nearly inseparable in practice and in reality.

## PROVIDING DOCUMENTATION

Documentation in integrative supervision probably does not differ from supervision conducted from other theoretical orientations, with a single departure. Supervisors maintain written notes of supervisory sessions, complete written evaluations as needed, and review supervisee's session notes, intake reports, and discharge reports (depending upon the clinical setting). All responsible positions come with the obligatory paperwork.

The sole departure lies in the integrative supervisor's insistence on concise documentation of the basis for treatment selection. Many intake reports proffer extensive descriptions of patient histories, health exams, and test results but eventuate in the identical treatment recommendation:

weekly individual psychotherapy. Or session notes obsess about specific clinical exchanges but lack any sense of treatment goals, directions, or outcomes. By contrast, much as with integrative assessment as described in Chapter 2 (this volume), we seek explication in clinical documentation of the multiple patient considerations that guide treatment selection.

Think of these as "when . . . then" formulations. *When* a patient presents with these diagnoses, goals, preferences, cultures, stages of change, and so on, *then* this therapy is indicated by the research evidence. If the bases of treatment recommendations were required in reports, then "the therapist's preferred theoretical orientation" would be embarrassingly recorded in many cases. This strikes to the heart of the integrative insistence on a systematic, evidence-based process of treatment selection responsive to the goals, preferences, personalities, and cultures of each individual.

## ADAPTING SUPERVISION

One of the most appealing (and effective) features of integrative psychotherapy is that an individualized treatment can be tailored to each client. A similar principle holds true for integrative supervision: An individualized supervision plan can be formulated for each trainee on the basis of his or her style, stage, preferences, experience, complexity, and other considerations. Just as we ask our students to behave multitheoretically and prescriptively in their clinical work, so too should we match our supervision to their unique needs and clinical strategies.

Integrative supervision will obviously take into account a number of trainee variables. Supervisors will assess personality characteristics, such as introversion versus extroversion or need for challenge versus need for support, and develop supervisory strategies that take these characteristics into account (Lampropoulos, 2003) to help the supervisee develop and discover his or her own voice. Although we cannot specify a priori all the possible supervisee variables and permutations of those variables, our supervision experience and the research literature (e.g., Holloway & Wampold, 1986; McNeill & Stoltenberg, 2016; Norcross & Halgin, 1997) suggest that we can improve supervision outcomes by tailoring it

to six trainee characteristics: supervisee preferences, developmental stage, therapy approach, cognitive style/reactance level, cultural identities, and clinical setting.

## Supervisee Preferences

As in clinical work, we try to elicit supervisees' expressed desires and genuine needs. And as with patients, we seriously consider supervisees' expressed desires but are not bound to them. They form the initial basis for our discussions and eventual supervision contract (as elaborated in Chapter 2, this volume).

Tactful questioning and sensitive inquiry can shed light on favored cognitive and interpersonal styles. How do you best tolerate feedback from others? What was your worst supervision experience like? How do you learn most effectively about psychotherapy? What sort of supervisory relationship works well for you? What do you hope to accomplish from our supervision sessions?

## Developmental Stage

A voluminous body of research demonstrates that supervisees grow through developmental levels (McNeill & Stoltenberg, 2016). Research suggests that certain supervisory styles are differentially effective for trainees at varying levels of experience. In the initial level, beginning students are highly motivated and highly dependent on their supervisors, whereas in the latter stage, advanced students seek more sophisticated formulations and are more attuned to individual differences among clients. One can immediately grasp that integrative supervision is oriented toward, and indicated for, advanced students, as we have repeatedly argued.

To oversimplify the developmental trajectory, beginning students are most interested in the acquisition of specific interviewing and therapy techniques; advanced practicum students seem more inclined toward the development of alternative formulations; interns tend to be most intrigued by examination of personal dynamics affecting therapy. A slightly different

formulation (Heppner & Roehlke, 1984) posits that beginning practicum students seek skills and support, moderately advanced trainees desire to expand their conceptual skills and theoretical knowledge, and even more advanced students express the desire to explore personal issues that might affect their ability to provide treatment. As with any stage model, the steps obviously overlap and the emphases are relative rather than absolute.

From such observations and research, we conclude that the goals of supervision should reflect the developmental stage of the trainee (Guest & Beutler, 1988). Supervisory goals should begin with considerable support and training in technical skill and progress to a consideration of more complex theoretical concepts, and finally endeavor to the work of solidifying and integrating theory and technique with personal response patterns. These later skills include special focus on interpersonal dynamics, particularly transference and countertransference. In oversimplified terms, students move from techniques to knowledge to self.

With experienced supervisees, I (JCN) strive for mutuality in psychotherapy supervision (Phillips & Kanter, 1984). The exchange is a process of mutual exploration and bidirectional exchanges. Although not abdicating my professional responsibilities or denying disparities in knowledge and power between us, I strive for an empathic and collaborative relationship. Such a relationship invigorates and inspires one to do more. Collaborative supervision is breathing new life into the old techniques and sometimes modifying a rigid approach that has become exhausting and unexciting to the experienced supervisee.

In another stage theory (Loganbill, Hardy, & Delworth, 1982), supervisees progress through three stages: stagnation, confusion, and integration. During the stagnation stage, the beginner is deceived by the illusion of simplicity in clinical work. The confusion stage follows, during which the trainee realizes that something is amiss and solutions seem elusive. Only later in training does the supervisee attain a sense of integration during which flexibility, security, and understanding emerge. Thus, the supervisor who impatiently expects the trainee to have attained integration early in training is likely to engender dismay, frustration, and diminished self-esteem.

I (LMP) certainly traversed these stages of supervisee development. Early on in supervision, I needed more hand-holding and direction. I was quiet and meek, seeking to learn but not confident enough in my abilities to actively participate. As I progressed as a therapist, I began participating more and found supervision to be stimulating. There is nothing as grand as the privilege to pick the brain of a seasoned therapist regarding a client. With clinical experience, I began to place the needs of the client beyond my own timidity and anxiety. I wanted to grow and become a better therapist.

Bottom line: Supervisees progress through a series of stages, and supervisors need to respond differentially to their respective levels of experience (Worthington, 1987). Of course, this is a cardinal integrative principle.

## Therapy Approach

We have already addressed how the methods of supervision typically mirror the methods of psychotherapy performed by the supervisee. This mirroring evolves into a more complex endeavor in integrative supervision when the supervisee conducts one form of psychotherapy for one client and another form of psychotherapy for another client: emotion-focused individual therapy for the 2:00 p.m. patient and then cognitive–behavioral group therapy at 3:00 p.m., for instance. Such frequent switches in psychotherapy methods and treatment formats probably require more energy, flexibility, and competence from the supervisee and the supervisor.

## Cognitive Style and Reactance Level

A body of research signifies that the conceptual level of the supervisee is another important consideration in fitting the supervision to the student. One aspect refers to students' level of conceptual complexity and includes their degree of self-initiative, ability to generate concepts, and tolerance for ambiguity (Handley, 1982). Students high in conceptual development benefit more from a self-directed instructional approach, whereas those lower in conceptual development perform better with externally oriented and externally controlled supervision.

An interpersonal trait of supervisees similar to cognitive style is *reactance*, the tendency to respond oppositionally to external direction and perceived authority. We reviewed reactance as a client variable earlier but it also emerges as a potent supervisee feature. Like the high-reactant client who is resistant to therapist directiveness, the high-reactant supervisee is likely to resist a directive supervisor. This student is likely to do best with a reflective and evocative supervisor who focuses on the student's experience and is less direct in recommending technical procedures (Tracey, Ellickson, & Sherry, 1989). This student is contrasted to the low-reactant student who is likely to respond well to supervisor directives.

How directive should a supervisor be? It depends. It depends on the supervisee's preferences, cognitive style, reactance level, and cultural identity.

## Cultural Identities

Much in the way that research has demonstrated that psychological services are enhanced by fitting them to the client's cultures (Bernal & Rodriguez, 2012), supervision is improved by adapting it to the supervisee's cultures. We respectfully ask supervisees which of their cultural identities—and the intersection of those multiple identities (Nettles & Balter, 2011)—are instrumental to their sense of self and their work in supervision (Inman & DeBoer Kreider, 2013). By *culture*, we refer to all salient dimensions of identity, such as chronological age, disability status, race and ethnicity, sexual orientation, gender, religion, and indigenous heritage.

We agree that all supervision is multicultural (Chopra, 2013) and try to explicitly adapt integrative supervision to those cultural identities nominated as salient by the trainee. Supervisees who feel their supervisors are culturally responsive experience a more productive supervision (Burkard et al., 2006). As a White, hetero, fully abled man occupying a privileged position in society and in supervision, I (JCN) need to pay particular attention to my potential ethnocentric biases.

The means of culturally adapting supervision are potentially infinite, but some of the more frequent have consisted of attending to language

choices, acknowledging the history of cultural imperialism in psychotherapy, collaborating with indigenous healers, addressing acculturation–separateness, and tracking for power-oppression dynamics in supervision. Two recent supervisees, one in a wheelchair and one a Muslim woman, taught me potent lessons about societal intolerance and my own precarious assumptions. The supervisor need not prove expert in all of these matters; rather, it is the supervisor's cultural awareness, willingness to learn, and cultural humility that approach the goal of cultural competence.

## Clinical Setting

In the prior chapter, we sketched how responsive supervision fits the clinical setting in which services are provided. Here we reiterate that point and urge supervisors not working in the same clinical environment as their supervisees to become knowledgeable about the clients, diagnoses, services, policies, documentations, and practices of that environment. Several accreditation standards and supervision guidelines require that supervisors be physically available on site for these and other reasons.

Responsively attending to these six supervisee characteristics—supervisee preferences, developmental stage, therapy approach, cognitive style/reactance level, cultural identity, and clinical setting—enables integrative supervisors to systematically and effectively personalize the supervision. The trick is to know which of these supervisee features are relevant in any given moment and which others are not of immediate import. The second trick is not to artificially force supervisees into any of these cookie-cutter molds; ongoing needs assessments and candid discussions will point to those that will fit the unique supervisee–supervisor dyad.

Even with similar cognitive styles and comparable training, each supervisee manifests an idiographic style. This style has been labeled as each trainee's *personal idiom* (Hogan, 1964), the unique meshing of personality and method. Supervisors who are attuned to these individualized styles can help the trainee use special attributes to benefit the therapy, obviously within appropriate limits. Supervisors who fail to recognize and appreciate each trainee's personalized approach, on the other

hand, will likely provoke considerable upset if the supervisor's own style is being unwittingly imposed on the trainee.

## MIXING SUPERVISION FORMATS

Integrative supervision is conducted in both individual and group formats. The former is devoted to supervision of individual cases and permits more intensive examination of video-recorded segments, individual evaluations, supervisee reactions, and those cringe-worthy moments we would all prefer not to share in a group of peers. The group supervision combines a myriad of pedagogical methods and team members. Representative examples include didactic presentations, reading assignments, discussion periods, personal modeling, group role plays, experiential activities, video demonstrations, case examples, and mini case conferences. The group supervision context provides trainees with an important opportunity to share their work with peers while at the same time taking advantage of the collected wisdom of their peers and the more advanced trainees who participate.

Following the integrative frame of *both/and*, we typically blend both individual and group supervision to capitalize on their respective strengths: group for efficiency and peer support, individual for sustained individual attention. As well, groups often create a cohesive community in which members learn vicariously from each other and serve informally as peer supervisors along the way. It takes a village to raise an integrative therapist.

# 4

# Structure and Process of Supervision

What happens in integrative supervision sessions? We answer this question by walking through the structure and process of sessions, relying extensively on case illustrations.

Not much can be said about a "typical" integrative session of supervision because so much is personalized to the individual supervisee, who, in parallel fashion, is personalizing treatment to the individual client. However, my (JCN) beginnings and endings are typical, almost routine. One astute trainee observed that "the bookends (start and finish) are the same, but in between never the same. It all just depends, doesn't it?" Exactly so.

## HOW INTEGRATIVE SUPERVISION TYPICALLY BEGINS

Individual supervision sessions, as a rule, commence with an exchange of pleasantries, my offer of water or diet soda (because I [JCN] am drinking one of them), usually a brief discussion of any residue or unfinished matters from the previous week, and sometimes a follow-up on a topic or skill we explored last week. Then, I ask, "Any clinically urgent matters today?" That directs us to any pressing or priority topics for the session. (With a few supervision sessions behind them, most trainees anticipate my question and start us on the path themselves.)

Advanced trainees typically create their own agenda for the session concordant with the supervision agreement. The supervisor will occasionally add an item to that agenda, such as explicit supervisee feedback on the supervision or a return to a skill deficit. Beginning students need more structure, so we cocreate the agenda and topics. The supervisor is more directive, consistent with the supervisee's developmental stage, but always collaborative.

The following snippet is taken from the beginning of one of our (LMP and JCN) supervision sessions. The supervisor asks how the supervisee is doing, how the end of the academic year is going. Supervisor asks about any urgent matters. Supervisee says yes. A client called in crisis. Supervisor asks if we have ever discussed that client before. Supervisee says no. Supervisor then inquires what else supervisee would like to talk about in the session, being mindful of the time. Supervisee replies that she also has video of a session in which she gathered client feedback about the success of treatment and another in which she shared the results of psychological testing with another client.

That's a typical interaction at the beginning of integrative supervision. We check about "clinical urgencies" and then the advanced trainee largely sets the agenda as he or she knows where he or she is getting stuck. Supervisor and supervisee have developed a comfort zone with each other. There are clear goals, a flexible agenda, a responsive relationship, and priority to urgent matters as they invariably pop up.

## CASE ILLUSTRATION: MULTIPLE HYPOTHESES

Integrative supervisors prize active construction of multiple hypotheses for clinical phenomena. Our rebellious, even subversive aims involve disrupting entrenched thinking and broadening the frame of reference. Instead of the supervisor's snap declaration of "Well, that's obviously X, Y, and Z" from the lens of a single theory, we opt for several plausible possibilities from the lens of informed pluralism.

This supervision segment delves further into the conflict first described in the previous chapter. In the transcript below, the supervisor (JCN) and the supervisee (LMP) watch a clip from her video-recorded therapy session during the past week. Thereafter, the supervisor observes:

**JCN:** Well, I think this is a wonderful moment. The patient is in conflict. So let's see you generate some hypotheses.

**LMP:** OK.

**JCN:** Let's start with her diagnostic profile.

**LMP:** OK.

**JCN:** She is scoring quite high (98/99) in avoidant, depressive, and dependent personality and also masochistic.

**LMP:** (Nodding)

**JCN:** Does that sound like it may apply to this patient?

**LMP:** Absolutely.

**JCN:** So, if she came out verbally that she didn't believe in this (pattern of results) and these tests, what might she be riddled with?

**LMP:** Guilt.

**JCN:** Guilt, yes. Fear of abandonment. That she is hurting you.

**LMP:** Right.

**JCN:** Her body seems to be saying one thing and verbally saying something quite different.

**LMP:** Right. And I don't realize that her body is saying that because I'm looking down at the paper.

**JCN:** Yes. Some of that is inevitable.

**LMP:** OK.

**JCN:** You seem pretty hard on yourself in this moment.

**LMP:** Well, because I am looking at this (videotape) saying, "Look up, look up—you're missing this!"

**JCN:** Right (chuckling).

**LMP:** Imagine I didn't have this videotape?

**JCN:** So an avoidant dependent person is in this perpetual cycle of anxiety. Wanting to be liked and loved and nurtured. And sometimes saying anything to avoid perceived rejection. That's one hypothesis.

**LMP:** Right.

**JCN:** Can you think of other hypotheses or alternatives that might explain this?

**LMP:** I think that she is also at odds with herself.

**JCN:** Beautifully put. . . .

In the integrative tradition, we believe in multiple causes and, of course, multiple perspectives to the clinical encounter. We endeavor to liberate supervisees from theoretical shackles and from becoming conceptually narrow. We look at the pluralistic reality. Asking for multiple hypotheses assists us in exploring different meanings; it helps us think inclusively and synthetically.

## CASE ILLUSTRATION: INTEGRATIVE FORMULATION AND TREATMENT ADAPTATION

In this video recording, the supervisee and supervisor discuss client preferences and treatment adaptations for a female college client. The supervisee (LMP), after watching the video of her therapy session, believed she

was too focused on her own agenda without sufficiently listening to the needs of the client. The supervisor (JCN) assures her that even though she may not have felt it was as fluid as she would have liked, she did indeed gain a respectable amount of useful information from the client to guide her future therapy. The supervisor assured the supervisee that the process of assessing client preferences and stages of change would become more natural and less of a checklist the more she incorporated the practice.

Indeed, after several more sessions with clients, I (LMP) found assessing preferences to be a seamless part of the intake session. It definitely became less of a checklist and more of a genuine desire to assess the desires of the individual. As said repeatedly, the aim of integrative supervision is to help people think integratively, not become mindless, flag-waving integrationists. This is exactly the process for me in training.

Here's our exchange from a supervision session devoted to integrative case formulation and treatment adaptation.

**JCN:** We'll stop it (the video of the supervisee's session with client) there.

**LMP:** Yes.

**JCN:** So, what's your sense or appraisal of that (the segment of videotaped therapy)?

**LMP:** Well, I think that I got everything in that I wanted to but that's also the problem. I wasn't listening to her (the client) enough. I had my own agenda going, like find out about homework, find out about this, find out about that. Instead of saying, "OK, what's happening? Are you OK?" She kept talking about how she wasn't sure. She was so anxious that I should have spent a little more time (focusing on her anxiety).

**JCN:** Sometimes when you are preoccupied with meeting your own lists it's hard to be present.

**LMP:** Yes.

**JCN:** At the same time, you got lots of material from her.

**LMP:** Yes.

**JCN:** You found out that she does want so-called homework assignments or between-session assignments. She's OK with the (lack of) meds as they are now.

**LMP:** Yes, she doesn't want meds.

**JCN:** Right. Just leave it where it is.

**LMP:** Right.

**JCN:** You've identified again that she brings that dependent, other-oriented pattern to everyone, including you.

**LMP:** Right.

**JCN:** That was a beautiful link: From (client saying) "I'm doing everything to please this boyfriend" to what she may be doing with you. (In the therapy video, the client talked about trying to please everyone. LMP then asked client how to discern if the client was trying to please the therapist in session. Client said she did not know.)

**LMP:** Right.

**JCN:** You brought the outside literally into the session.

**LMP:** Yeah.

**JCN:** As you address her pleasing behavior and she continues to resolve it, you will see improvement in both areas.

**LMP:** Yeah. I think part of it was that I was feeling like I had to get it all in because we don't have that much more time to meet. (Client was a senior in college, and it was nearing the end of the semester.) So she came in last time in crisis, and this was the second time I was seeing her. I wanted to make sure I was filling her needs and, by doing that and running the checklist, I'm afraid that maybe I didn't. . . .

**JCN:** Yes. And you will become more fluid after a while—where you balance both getting the most information to tailor treatment and listening closely to her. But the first couple of times it seems like most of our attention is focused on gathering information.

**LMP:** Yeah.

**JCN:** You did make wonderful links on how it was all going.

**LMP:** OK.

**JCN:** In fact, I wrote down several instances (grabbing his notes from the table).... You obtained her preferences. She wants to meet every week. And yes, it all feels a little urgent because she comes in crisis and you have, what, possibly 5 more weeks (until the client graduates)?

**LMP:** No, not even.

**JCN:** Not even. And you also ascertained that she is indecisive as part of her anxiety.

**LMP:** Trying to be a people pleaser.

**JCN:** Yes, and in the extreme, a dependent personality perhaps. So, you got lots of material. And she seemed to respond quite well to you.

**LMP:** Yes, I hope.

(We spent a minute discussing the client's probable diagnoses as one way of tailoring treatment; that part of the exchange is excluded here.)

**JCN:** Did you feel more comfortable asking the client for her preferences during the session?

**LMP:** Oh yeah. I felt definitely more comfortable than I have, but I still don't feel like it is fluid enough. Especially when I'm watching it.

**JCN:** (Nodding in the affirmative)

**LMP:** I think that it is a little disjointed. I could have paused more, reflected back, and then moved on. Instead of rushing to obtain the information (for treatment planning).

**JCN:** You feel like you didn't do enough empathic connections....

**LMP:** Right.

**JCN:** Well, I found three of them (in the session segment just watched)... judging by her body language and her verbal response. When you said,

"You seem to be struggling between what you need and what he needs or wants," she immediately said, "Yes, that's exactly it."

**LMP:** (Nodding)

**JCN:** Then she came forward and said she was indecisive. Afterwards, she said she would like homework (between sessions) and meeting every week, and you agreed to that. That's another form of empathy and understanding preferences.

**LMP:** Uh hum.

**JCN:** I got the sense that she felt grateful for that.

**LMP:** OK.

**JCN:** If you were to improve upon anything other than "make sure you get all the information on the checklist," what else would that be?

(We discuss the patient dynamics for about another minute.)

**JCN:** So, if we go down the list (the treatment adaptation list, starting with diagnoses).... Now I'm creating the mistake you just said you made (smiling about following the list). Here's a client with an adjustment disorder, maybe a dependent personality disorder, some anxiety, if not of clinical severity at least her coping style. And she's indecisive.

**LMP:** (Nodding)

**JCN:** She wants action (stage), she wants homework, and she wants a therapy session every week.

**LMP:** (Nodding) Uh hum.

**JCN:** That was a lot of information to get in what, 2 minutes?

**LMP:** Right; it didn't take very long.

**JCN:** So, it was efficient, it was effective. When you're inside your head saying, "Now make sure I ask all the questions I've read about," I understand that you're preoccupied.

**LMP:** OK.

**JCN:** I saw no evidence that she (the patient) was distracted (in the session). In fact, three times you seemed to hit it right there.

**LMP:** OK. Good.

**JCN:** (Nodding) In going forward, do you feel comfortable and competent in offering her preferred form of therapy?

**LMP:** I think so, yes.

**JCN:** For the action stage, you mentioned "cognitive–behavioral" (referring to the treatment method that the supervisee plans to use with this client).

**LMP:** Right.

**JCN:** And she's comfortable with homework; you gave her several homework suggestions.

**LMP:** (Nodding)

**JCN:** Cognitive–behavioral therapy and no medications at this point.

**LMP:** And she wants me to be more directive.

**JCN:** Yes.

(After this segment, the supervision dyad considers the supervisee's countertransference to the client.)

This segment focuses on the supervisee's new efforts to assess and accommodate patient preferences and stages and how the process will evolve from a technical endeavor to a seamless and relational one with additional practice. The supervisee articulates the common conflict between staying relationally attuned with the patient and the process, on the one hand, and efficiently collecting the necessary information on the patient's transdiagnostic features, on the other. A difficult dialectical balance, even with considerable practice.

The supervisor attempts to support the supervisee and soothe her anxiety about her perceived imperfections in the session. It comprises a mix of reflecting and affirming, Socratic questioning, inviting supervisee self-reflection, offering support and reassurance, and pointing out supervisee's

successes despite her performance anxiety. Again, there was an unspoken understanding and shorthand vocabulary between the supervisor and supervisee.

In the end, the session illustrates a representative slice of integrative supervision in which an advanced student gathers the necessary transdiagnostic patient information to arrive at a preliminary case formulation and to adapt treatment accordingly. That treatment plan is based, in this instance, on the time parameters (a few more sessions), the patient's diagnoses, stated preferences, stage of change, and, in the subsequent discussion, the supervisee's countertransference potential. Systematically tailoring psychotherapy to even one of those transdiagnostic characteristics—preferences, stages of change—has been shown to demonstrably improve the efficacy and efficiency of the treatment (see Chapter 2, this volume, for the research evidence). And responsiveness to the patient's goals and temporal limits is supported by decades of clinical experience and less formalized research.

## CASE ILLUSTRATION: PARALLEL PROCESS

In this video-recorded exchange, supervision attends to the parallel process between the supervisee's therapy session with her client and the supervision session. Parallel process, in its traditional definition, constitutes a reenactment of the therapeutic situation in the supervisory relationship (Grey & Fiscalini, 1987). In this example of the parallel process, the client (whom we have given the pseudonym of Melanie) exposes her vulnerabilities to her therapist, and LMP, in supervision, is sharing her vulnerabilities with her supervisor (JCN).

**JCN:** In the tape we are about to watch, you were a little anxious?

**LMP:** Um hmm.

**JCN:** She was avoidant completing the psychological testing, and you don't have much practice giving feedback on the testing results.

**LMP:** Yes. She agreed to most of what I read, but that may just be her avoiding....

**JCN:** Yes. We also see her dependency personality score is 100. (Chuckling) ... So she may be agreeing because of her dependency need or avoiding perceived rejection or abandonment.

**LMP:** Um hmm.

**JCN:** A difficult call. And yet, she's been strong enough with her feedback to give you less than optimal ratings and to redirect you a bit. (In previous sessions, the client provided the therapist with feedback in areas that she thought could be improved in therapy. These included the therapist being more directive and pushing the client to discuss issues that she purposefully avoided.)

**LMP:** Right.

**JCN:** That speaks well to your therapy relationship with her. She can tell you things that are less than pleasant. Do you have that experience?

**LMP:** Yes. My fear is that I'm getting sucked into her pattern of moving forward and then pushing back. And I'm not being assertive enough.

**JCN:** Assertive and directive enough to focus on that particular pattern?

**LMP:** Yes.

**JCN:** Well, I'm mindful, Leah, as you present this (therapy segment) to me perhaps you are doing something like Melanie. You are willing to show less than an optimal therapy experience. I want to congratulate you.

**LMP:** Thank you.

**JCN:** I distinctly recall trying to hide in supervision what I thought were the not-the-best things I had done in therapy sessions for fear of rebuke or that I wasn't supposed to be doing that.

**LMP:** Well, I'm fearful; this is an area where I clearly need direction.

**JCN:** Your inexperience trumps the fear of disclosing part of the session that didn't go well?

**LMP:** Oh, sure. And the hope that it doesn't happen again the next time I have to give (testing) feedback.

**JCN:** That speaks well for you. And I'm glad you are feeling increasingly open and sharing (in supervision). I do understand the evaluation anxiety of not presenting things that didn't go well. I think that as our alliance, much like your alliance with Melanie, improves over time, we can successfully address the pattern. All right: Do you want to watch it (the videotape)?

**LMP:** Yes!

A lot of material and process transpired in this brief exchange. One item of note concerns the mutual recognition of parallel process in which the dynamic transpiring in the therapy session with the client is reenacted in the supervision session. The client expressed her vulnerabilities in therapy just as her therapist did in supervision. Both the supervisor and therapist should remain alert for that pattern deepening into chronic self-denigration. Another point is that the supervisor affirmed and congratulated the supervisee for expressing vulnerability and sharing her less-than-best work in supervision. Following this exchange, the supervisee verbalized her wish that she had done likewise with her client. Still another is the supervisor's self-disclosure that he had purposefully hidden his weak work from his clinical supervisors.

Astute supervisors, integrative and otherwise, remain attuned to what is not revealed and not communicated in supervision. Within a single supervision session, 84% of trainees reported withholding information from their supervisors. The most common nondisclosures involved a negative supervision experience and a perceived poor clinical example. Better supervisory alliances and lower trainee anxiety led to greater willingness to disclose in supervision (Mehr, Ladany, & Caskie, 2010).

In addition to cultivating the relationship and lowering trainee anxiety, supervisors can consider addressing the topic during initial meetings, self-disclosing their own experiences and temptations of nondisclosure, and raising the propensity periodically during supervision. Wondering aloud about what supervisees would wish to hide, avoid, or not disclose has served us well as a nonthreatening invitation.

## CASE ILLUSTRATION: TERMINATION WORK

In this excerpt, LMP just finished showing JCN a video of a termination session with a long-term client. In the therapy session she asked the client to share with her those things that worked well throughout the course of treatment and those things that the therapy could have done without. The client responds that he was happy the therapist did not push him to do out-of-therapy homework. Discussing the session with LMP, JCN pointed out that the client is telling her that had she not adapted to his preferences, he would have stopped treatment.

**JCN:** You could see his (the client's) pleasure and his gratitude throughout the session. I know you have other upcoming termination sessions in which you will have opportunities to ask what worked and what did not. The client got a lot out of the therapy. Especially when he talked about if he could go back and look at his freshman self.

**LMP:** And that is so profound for me to hear because it was a struggle early on. There were things that I had said, like it won't always be this way. And he would say I want to believe you, but I don't.

**JCN:** Yes (nodding).

**LMP:** To hear him say that and validate the things that I thought....

**JCN:** Yes. You can get a little moist hearing that, yes?

**LMP:** Yeah. It reminds me why I do what I do, I guess. In a big way.

**JCN:** It is one of those wonderful moments. And you may have missed the immediate connection, but he essentially said if you hadn't honored his preferences and heard what he needed, he would have dropped out.

**LMP:** Yep. And that is twofold: One that we (supervision dyad) had not been meeting yet so I didn't know to act on his preferences for things like homework. Another is my inability if they come in and don't do homework (a goal from a previous session), then I don't push them.

**JCN:** Well, a lot of this matching is done intuitively. And you read somehow that pushing him may have violated what he needed and perhaps may have even damaged your therapeutic relationship.

**LMP:** Yeah.

**JCN:** The impressive research on incorporating preferences when clinically and ethically indicated tells us exactly that. The dropout rate, on average, is one-third less when you accommodate patient preferences. He just handed that to you.

**LMP:** Yeah.

**JCN:** And dropouts are one of those things that you don't discover until it is too late. But if you had pushed the homework, he may have dropped out.

**LMP:** Yes (nodding).

This supervision excerpt underscores several important points about therapy termination and its review in integrative supervision. In therapy sessions, we routinely ask therapists to discuss candidly with clients what did and did not work in treatment, acknowledge the success with clients, cherish the gains, and collect those answers for self-reflection and future guidance in clinical work. In supervision sessions, we try to connect the early-session assessment and adaptation of client preferences (and stages, reactance, culture, etc.) to subsequent therapy outcomes, integrate the clinical results with the research findings, and, of course, frame it all within termination work.

In this instance, accommodating the patient's preferences proved decisive. Although it was clear LMP was responding intuitively to what her client needed, asking for preferences cuts through imprecise intuition, provides direct answers from clients, and solidifies the therapy alliance. We are both certain that we have lost clients in the past, despite our best intentions, because we did not systematically inquire and privilege their preferences, cultures, stages of change, and the like. We were not on the same page.

## HOW INTEGRATIVE SUPERVISION TYPICALLY ENDS

Five or 10 minutes before the end of the scheduled 50 minutes, the supervisor typically announces the remaining time and begins to wrap up the session. Usually there is some summary of what has been addressed or

gained during the supervision and then an invitation to reflect on what is tentatively planned for the subsequent meeting. As the supervisor scribbles a summary note, he or she records what is anticipated for the next supervision, as frequently will the supervisee. A representative entry might read, "Next week: Videotape on feeling stuck in C's ambivalence; review of session notes; practice assessing the stages of change." Or for the week after that: "Next week: Reading on MI [motivational interviewing] methods; videotape on assessing stages; countertransference toward F; 30th session supervisee feedback." I (JCN) jot down between two and four matters to create some structure to our session and to remind us of our respective responsibilities.

As a supervisee, I (LMP) have found comfort in knowing we will recap the central points of our supervisory session. Not only does it highlight the aspects of supervision that JCN believes were important but it also allows us to discuss anything that we may have missed while knee deep in the session. Our supervision sessions tend to fly by in what feels like an instant. During these times I sometimes fail to bring up a matter I wanted to discuss. Preserving time at the end of the session has largely prevented me from missing it. In another intentional manifestation of parallel process, I now use a similar process in therapy. Before wrapping up I summarize the session and ask about our mutual expectations for the following session and the time in between (out-of-session work). This also permits clients to discuss anything they wanted to but have not.

Lately, I (JCN) have been working toward realizing two goals at the end of each supervision session, which probably says more about the particular supervisor than integrative supervision. First, I am more aware of and bound to the time limits. Especially while watching video, I enjoy the experience and frequently lose track of time. I am committed to better maintaining the time frame. Second, at the end of each session I inquire informally of the supervisee's comfort and confidence in implementing the particular skill we practiced. A quick, "You good with that?" or "Feel comfortable doing that in the next session?" provides a check on the supervisee's reception and experience. I have learned that doing so tempers my enthusiasm for integrative work, which occasionally blinds me to its implementation challenges for supervisees.

# 5

# Handling Common Supervisory Challenges

Supervisory challenges are no more or less prevalent in integrative supervision than in other forms of supervision, but they tend to differ. In this chapter, we concern ourselves with several of these challenges—difficult supervisees, trainee impairment, power and evaluation, diversity issues, legal/ethical matters, and conflict management—with added attention to the distinctive twists confronted in integrative supervision.

## DEALING WITH "DIFFICULT" SUPERVISEES

A virtue of aging (or academic seniority) is that fewer onerous tasks are dumped in one's lap. That is certainly the case with clinical supervision and me (JCN). Although I continue to supervise students across the entire spectrum of clinical experience, most of my supervision is now conducted of my own volition and with advanced trainees of my choosing. That has

http://dx.doi.org/10.1037/15967-005
*Supervision Essentials for Integrative Psychotherapy*, by J. C. Norcross and L. M. Popple
Copyright © 2017 by the American Psychological Association. All rights reserved.

reduced the number of "difficult" and impaired trainees I supervise. In truth, I now typically select my own trainees from self-referred doctoral students on internship, postdoctoral psychologists seeking supervised experience for licensure, and seasoned mental health professionals seeking training in integrative therapy.

To be sure, intrinsically difficult supervisees exist, just as do difficult, rigid supervisors. A negative supervisory experience may indeed be attributable to a problematic trainee, but let us too entertain the possibility that the problem is due to a rigid supervisory style or counterproductive events in supervision (Gray, Ladany, Walker, & Ancis, 2001). One such example occurs when a supervisor dismisses a trainee's thoughts and feelings. Another issue is a dogmatic, authoritarian supervisory style, as mentioned previously. Research documents that counterproductive supervisory events commonly lead to a weakening of the supervisory relationship and a diminishment of the work with the client (Ramos-Sánchez et al., 2002).

In our experience, the three principal difficult types of supervisees encountered in integrative supervision are (a) trainees verbally professing interest in integrative work but behaviorally resisting efforts to supervise them doing just that; (b) trainees unable "to be different" with different clients; and (c) trainees suffering from unremitting perfectionism, of whom integrative work seems to attract a disproportionate percentage.

The word is steadily spreading to mental health educators about the wisdom and the pragmatics of integrative supervision. Although experienced faculty increasingly appreciate integrative training, they are sometimes surprised to encounter resistance in their students about such prospects. Even in the earliest stages of graduate training, students often come with theoretical biases that limit their openness. It proves surprising and disconcerting for an integrative supervisor to meet with trainees who praise and seek supervision of integrative work but who subsequently resist said supervision.

We suspect a profound conflict between intellect and anxiety in these instances. Intellectually, the supervisees appreciate the value and efficacy of broader training but hold on to a restricted monotherapy for security and anxiety reduction. They understand the need for more pluralistic treatments responsive to clients, but they are bound by their theory and

entropy. Their conflict reminds us of a line from Kafka: "I am in chains. Don't touch my chains."

Genuine acceptance of an integrative perspective in supervision tends to vary as a function of the strength of the supervisee's previous theoretical allegiance. An integrative supervision is readily accepted, indeed obvious, to trainees not indoctrinated into a single camp or "school." By contrast, advanced students indoctrinated in one system can experience considerable difficulty in overcoming their loyalty and lethargy (Norcross, 1986). Deviations are experienced as betrayal or confusion or vulnerability; the process is akin to separation anxiety in which early separation results in anxiety and the trainees return to the omniscient "mother" theory for support and security. Having located their comfortable niche in the psychotherapy morass, these inveterate students are satisfied with their treasured proficiency and are less than motivated, for the most part, to expand their therapeutic repertoire. Robertson (1979) tellingly observed that many trainees with previously established competencies in one psychotherapy orientation want to become more proficient in that orientation, despite claims to the contrary.

In these circumstances, we generally delay introducing the integrative possibilities until the supervisee's anxiety dissipates, conduct the supervision within the trainees' favored theoretical tradition with an occasional addition of a method from another theoretical tradition (assimilative integration), and/or refer the trainee to another supervisor. A participant in an integrative workshop I (JCN) was conducting once quipped that the supervisor's options were to "wait, bait, or trade."

A related, but conceptually distinct, type of "difficult" trainees comprises those willing to work integratively but unable "to be different" with different clients. For example, some therapists (such as JCN) are naturally more animated and evocative in their interpersonal style; these individuals can use this natural style to conduct therapy in which they take a more active role. In contrast, those (such as LMP) whose personal style is naturally quieter and less active may work best with a therapeutic approach that is more serene and less energized. Each cluster of supervisees (and all those in between) expectedly find their personal styles and idioms more

amenable to some treatment methods and relationship stances than to others.

Here's the rub: Integration desires that supervisees acquire, at the same time, a flexible, multitheoretical repertoire and an individual clinical style that fits them best. Most students can accommodate both in harmony, but some cannot. Supervisors who try to coerce a change in personality or style generate trainees who feel like they are enacting a script that never seems right. Attempts to coach, persuade, and model a different relational or technical stance meet with supervisee frustration, resistance, or temporary behavior change followed by a drift back to baseline behavior.

These students present with narrow ranges that fit them but not many clients. The root problems may involve pervasive anxiety, relational inflexibility, or rigid conceptualization of psychotherapy. The latter seems to be closely related to *myside bias* in which supervisees evaluate evidence, generate examples, and test hypotheses in a manner automatically biased toward their own prior attitudes, such as a single school of therapy (Stanovich, West, & Toplak, 2013). The concern is not intelligence but rigidity.

In these circumstances, the supervisor's candid feedback typically produces immediate agreement and relief on the part of the supervisee. Not all clinicians can acquire or retain such breadth and flexibility. We retreat to the less ambitious model of integrative supervision (see Chapter 2): single-system competence and systematic referral.

A third genre of a "difficult" supervisee involves the perfectionist who is drawn to the comprehensiveness and idealism of psychotherapy integration. Although perfectionism is found in trainees of all theoretical stripes (Arkowitz, 2001), we are convinced that integration attracts a larger share (but concede we have no empirical evidence for the assertion). An obsessive desire to pull together the major systems of psychotherapy, the ambitious quest for the holy grail of fitting each patient to the optimal treatment, and the zealous devotion to the craft all represent the upsides of perfectionism. But the downsides manifest early and often in supervision as well: impatience with the progress of clients and themselves, excessive fear of

therapeutic failure and exposure of their vulnerabilities to authority figures, and the chronic anxiety of never performing well enough. Perfectionist supervisees bring a decidedly mixed bag of traits.

In these circumstances, we generously acknowledge the positive features of the perfectionist traits, gently identify the supervision-interfering behaviors, and mutually target them for improvement in both the therapy and supervision sessions. Should the perfectionism manifest severely, then we strongly recommend a course of (integrative!) personal therapy.

## TRAINEE DEFICITS

Integrative supervisors—well, at least these integrative supervisors—assume that we all have more to learn and that skill deficits are universal. It's only a matter of the degree of skill deficit and whether that deficit seriously compromises the health and treatment of clients. In this respect, all supervisees present with skill deficits, and the less experienced supervisees evince more skill detriments. Research confirms less experienced supervisees are more likely to seek help to overcome their deficits and are thus less resistant than are their more experienced counterparts (Bernard & Goodyear, 2014).

Skill deficits in trainees can be broken down into three main categories: interpersonal, technical, and conceptual (Ladany, Friedlander, & Nelson, 2005). Technical and conceptual deficits are usually easier to overcome than interpersonal skills because they can be mastered through course work, instruction, observation, and didactics. These skills are what most would consider the meat of psychotherapy: assessment, intervention, case conceptualization, testing, referrals, and the like.

Students lacking in interpersonal skills prove a challenge for all supervisors but perhaps more so for integrative supervisors. You will recall that we are supervising advanced graduate students in tailoring their interpersonal behaviors and technical methods to each client; if those students do not yet possess the fundamental interpersonal skills, then we cannot, and do not, proceed to asking them to adapt their level of directiveness, mode of empathy, and overall style of relating. You cannot tailor what you do not yet possess.

In these circumstances, we immediately turn to teaching and modeling basic helping skills and, in the most deficient of students, cease integrative work altogether. The remediation plan takes different directions contingent upon the particulars but usually requires supervisees to complete interpersonal skills training and practica-to-competence, not simply the end of the semester. More often than not, I (JCN) express to deficient trainees my chagrin at not working together in integrative supervision as planned, and I apologize for the gaps in a training system that did not properly teach and/or evaluate them before sending them onto more advanced training. Their deficits are iatrogenic results of feeble screening of interpersonal acumen during graduate admissions and of the dearth of competency-based training.

Unfortunately, some trainees will not benefit from any extended amount of training or remediation. Nor would they be fit for the profession after an infinite amount of training. Most training programs enroll students with problems of professional competence (Jacobs et al., 2011). Like it or not, supervisors serve as gatekeepers to the profession. Supervisors assume the ethical responsibility—to the clients for whom they assume responsibility, to their supervisees, and to the profession—to communicate with the graduate program or licensing board the deficits they believe a supervisee is unable to overcome (Jacobs et al., 2011). This can be a difficult dialogue but an essential one.

Of course, not all interpersonal skill deficiencies are so severe or compromising. In the spirit of "we all have deficits and are learning," we model, identify, teach, and practice, frequently with rating and training forms for the respective skills. We try to model an appropriate interpersonal environment in supervision for them with their clients. We identify the precise interpersonal skills lacking, normalizing the deficit (when appropriate) and the emotions the supervisee may feel as a result (embarrassment, shame, guilt). It is our mistakes, certainly not our successes, from which we learn. We teach specific skills, practice them in supervision, and use standardized rating forms to assess and reach minimum levels of proficiency. Virtually all interpersonal skills can be learned to a modest level of competence (Norcross, 2011).

## POWER AND EVALUATION

Power in the supervisory relationship inevitably confers responsibility to evaluate, grade, direct, and enhance supervisees throughout their training and growth. The position cannot be taken lightly, as a routine activity or another class to teach. Client lives and supervisee careers are at stake.

An abuse of that power is detrimental and unethical at any stage of training, but more so at the beginning when the student typically lacks confidence in his or her clinical abilities and has not yet fully internalized the role of healer. I (LMP) frequently recall my integrative supervisor (JCN) looking puzzled and asking me, usually after watching video of my therapy sessions, why I was not more warm and expressive. He would ask variants of the question, "Leah, why are you not in session like you are in supervision?" I did not know I could be! I was taught by a powerful supervisor early in my training to keep emotion at bay. The injunction was to be a blank slate, disengage from the client. This early insistence on a single way of relating to clients hindered my relational abilities as a clinician, and I struggle to this day to consistently let the warmer, engaging me emerge in session.

Supervision based on mutual respect and shared responsibility reduces power struggles and soothes evaluation anxieties—so do personal support, clear communication of expectations, and the conviction that mistakes (except gross ethical violations) prove unavoidable. The evaluation process (see Chapter 2) is largely open and transparent; supervisee difficulties are known and addressed in ongoing formative feedback well before any formal summative evaluation is completed. The collective vibe helps form a confidence within the supervisee and in interaction with other professionals.

That is not to say that the supervisor has lost control. The integrative supervisor maintains responsibility and control but relinquishes the need to govern the entire agenda or interaction. Sometimes the supervisor needs to be in the front of the boat actively steering and propelling, but with advanced students, the supervisor usually leads better from the back of the boat as a first mate. That's frequently the difference between dreading an hour put aside each week for supervision and looking forward to enhancing one's clinical effectiveness and professional development.

## MULTICULTURAL DIVERSITY

Integrative supervisors enthusiastically embrace multiculturalism. It's a natural and necessary extension of the integrative prizing of individual differences to broader cultural differences. Vive la différence! Integration posits that the context for every individual—African, Asian, Latino, or Anglo; straight, gay, bisexual, or trans; Muslim, Christian, Jew, or atheist—is unique. And each supervision needs to be constructed to match the needs of a particular trainee. Culture is one essential way to do that.

In parallel form, supervisees are expected and taught to culturally tailor psychotherapy to their clients. As reviewed earlier, the research attests that cultural adaptations demonstrably improve treatment outcomes. Particularly effective are orienting treatment to a specific cultural group (instead of a variety of cultural backgrounds), conducting therapy in the client's native language (Smith, Rodriguez, & Bernal, 2011), and avoiding translators in sessions whenever possible (Paniagua, 2005).

Single-school therapies, particularly those born of a dominant "father" and rooted in a culture-bound theory of personality, tend to subtly maintain White, androcentric, Western European, heterosexual norms. We now rightfully view many of the single-school "universal" principles as instances of clinical myopia or cultural imperialism. Integrative supervision, by contrast, relies on neither a particular founder nor a theory of personality. Our sole "universal" principle is that people and cultures differ and should be treated as such. No wonder that virtually every feminist, multicultural, and culturally responsive theory describes itself as integrative in practice.

Nonetheless, most students arrive for integrative supervision unprepared for cultural adaptations, either in supervision or in therapy. This should not come as a surprise: Much of what supervisees learn about multicultural diversity comes from books or through a professor teaching the subject matter. Even then, the majority of trainees do not believe multicultural topics were meaningfully integrated into their courses (Constantine, Ladany, Inman, & Ponterotto, 1996), and an overwhelming majority of doctoral students perceive themselves as not competent in multicultural matters following graduation (Allison, Crawford, Echemendia, Robinson, & Knepp, 1994).

Supervisors thus have a vital responsibility to help supervisees bridge the gap between theory and practice in multiculturalism (Chopra, 2013). Integrative supervisors can do so by modeling and manifesting cultural sensitivity within supervision sessions and by teaching and tracking supervisees culturally adapting services to their clients. The ability of supervisors to model appropriate interventions as well as acknowledge their own limitations multiculturally helps students develop their multicultural competence (Inman & Ladany, 2014). All supervisors can contribute by advocating diverse experiences that train students to serve clients from historically undertreated groups, by undergoing diversity training themselves, by sharing their concerns and limitations of diversity competence with supervisees, and by including cultural competencies as part of the evaluation criteria.

In our supervisee evaluations, we assess cultural and identity benchmarks adapted from competency benchmarks in professional psychology (Fouad et al., 2009). We measure the supervisee's awareness, sensitivity, and skills working with diverse individuals, groups, and communities. We track the supervisee's ability to independently monitor and apply knowledge of the self as shaped by diversity, others shaped by diversity, the interaction of the self and others shaped by diversity, and applications based on individual and cultural context. As well, we assess supervisees' ability to understand and monitor their own cultural identity in relation to clinical work and whether they critically evaluate feedback and initiate consultation when uncertain about diversity concerns that invariably arise.

## LEGAL AND ETHICAL MATTERS

Integrative supervisors bear the same legal and ethical responsibilities as their colleagues. Any health professional supervising a trainee "practicing" on his or her license has certainly felt the weight (and scare) of poor outcomes. Indeed, failure to supervise properly emerges as one of the top 10 causes of disciplinary actions by regulatory boards against psychologists (Pope & Vasquez, 2016). Let the master beware (Sacuzzo, 2003).

What appears distinctive to integrative supervision are the murky ethical dilemmas when single-system supervisees are disinclined or refuse

to relinquish clients for whom another approach has been repeatedly and empirically shown to be demonstrably better suited (Norcross, Beutler, & Clarkin, 1990). The dilemma highlights a number of ethical sensitivities and research complexities. The ethics codes of all mental health professions dictate that practitioners should employ the most efficacious and efficient treatments identified by the best available research, clinical expertise, and in accordance with client values, cultures, and preferences. But defining what constitutes a more effective treatment bogs down in multiple evidentiary questions (according to the research? the therapist? the client?), disparate research designs (only randomized controlled trials? generalizable but less controlled outcome studies?), and even interpretation of the same outcome research (what constitutes "demonstrably better?"). No professional consensus exists on these questions, and thus no universal judgments can be rendered.

Here's what we conclude, from a research-informed integrative position. First, consensually and empirically discredited practices should not be routinely offered. Second, treatment methods and relational stances that compellingly improve therapy outcomes for certain patients should be routinely offered, probably insisted upon, by integrative supervisors.

Regarding the former, robust professional consensus has been achieved on the discreditation of dozens of treatment methods and psychological tests for youth and adults (e.g., Koocher, McMann, Stout, & Norcross, 2015; Lilienfeld, 2007; Norcross, Koocher, & Garofalo, 2006). Absent an unusual circumstance, such as a client insisting on that particular treatment, we as integrative supervisors instruct trainees not to provide discredited treatments. An occasional supervisee will protest that such a treatment (e.g., Orgone box, primal scream, magnet therapy, crystal healing) lies within his or her competence and that it has worked before (usually for the supervisee him- or herself). We handle this supervisory conflict as outlined in the next section and also address it as an ethical and legal matter. Practitioners should not, ethically or legally, provide treatment considered by professional consensus and research evidence to be discredited or potentially harmful when alternative treatments exist. *Primum non nocere* (Latin for "First, do no harm").

Regarding the latter, psychotherapy research has now progressed to the point where certain relational behaviors and therapy–client matches have been shown to work demonstrably better than the alternatives. We do not refer here to Treatment Method A for Diagnosis B but rather to relational behaviors (e.g., alliance, empathy, goal consensus, collecting feedback) and the fit to transdiagnostic client features (e.g., reactance level, stages of change, patient preferences, culture). The supervisory challenge—and controversy—concern the boundary of demonstrably better outcomes. When the research results are not consistent or compelling, we encourage advanced supervisees to follow their personal style and idiom. But when the cumulative research is consistent and compelling, we insist on that course of action. That's the ethical and legal mandate: Prioritize the clinical care of a patient over the comfort and preferences of trainees (or supervisors).

## HANDLING CONFLICTS

In integrative supervision, we cultivate multiple hypotheses, expect rich differences in perspectives, and promote free exchanges of ideas. Differences need not turn into conflicts. This shift is more than semantically relabeling "conflict" into "differences"; embracing and valuing differences lie at the heart of integration. Most differences turn out to be complementary, rather than contradictory, when embedded within a pluralistic frame and when tailored to individual client and supervisee differences.

In making final decisions on how to act, we do experience a certain amount of conflict in supervision, but far less than do most of our colleagues. Our sense, buttressed by research (e.g., Robiner, Fuhrman, & Ristvedt, 1993), is that evaluation is the most common area for conflict to occur in supervision (Friedlander, 2015). Even here, as described a few pages ago, a transparent and explicit process seems to diminish surprise or conflict.

Over the years, I (JCN) have reflected on the paucity of conflict in integrative supervision and regularly queried supervisees on their take. The relative absence of rancor seems to occur as a function of carefully selecting my supervisees, crafting together a written contract for supervision, providing frequent formative feedback, requesting formal feedback

from the trainee, and initiating honest discussions throughout. If a supervisee is ever surprised by my written evaluation, then I slipped in completing one of these tasks.

Supervisees mention the regular feedback and written contract as well, but they appear to experience it as more relational. Their recent observations include, "There is nothing to push back on"; "You were supportive and flexible from day one"; "You assumed that I was competent and that we all have a few cracks"; "We discussed and hashed that out earlier"; "You encouraged me to develop my own style within the treatment selection, so where would be the conflict?"

When conflicts do occur in supervision, we try to address them immediately and overtly. Neglecting or mismanaging conflict proves dangerous to the supervision process (M. L. Nelson, Barnes, Evans, & Triggiano, 2008). Most conflict between supervisees and supervisor can be and should be resolved in one supervision session (Bernard & Goodyear, 2014). The longer a conflict takes to resolve, the more detrimental it will probably prove to the relationship (Safran & Muran, 2000).

We try to handle conflicts in supervision in much the same nondefensive way as we teach supervisees to approach a conflict or rupture with clients in psychotherapy; that is, remain calm and curious, respond nondefensively, perhaps express appreciation for the client's honesty, attend directly to the relationship, adjust behavior as indicated, and collect feedback on the process in that session and in a future session (Safran, Muran, & Eubanks-Carter, 2011). Training students in such rupture resolution improves their clients' outcomes ($d = 0.52$ vs. no training; Safran et al., 2011).

In this way, the supervisor turns conflict into a learning experience for the supervisee and models conflict resolution skills. The ability of supervision to recover from conflicts in the relationship tends to strengthen the supervisory alliance and the supervision experience as a whole. This is seen as the tear–repair process (Bordin, 1983). Successful conflict resolution in supervision gives the supervisee a platform to resolve conflicts with his or her own clients in a healthy and effective manner (Friedlander, 2015; M. I. Nelson, 2008). Likewise, if a rupture is not resolved, supervisees may then mime the conflict with their clients in an attempt to resolve the original conflict with their supervisors (Arkowitz, 2001).

Perhaps no place speaks more to the strength of the supervisory alliance than trainees feeling comfortable enough to place concerns and conflicts on the supervision table. It speaks to the trust that the supervisor will not retaliate against them in the form of evaluations, grades, or negative feedback. Research suggests, however, that supervisees are far less likely than supervisors to bring up conflicts (Ladany, Hill, Corbett, & Nutt, 1996).

The developmental stage, cognitive complexity, and reactance style of supervisees influence the conflict resolution process. Less experienced supervisees typically need more teaching and support, whereas more experienced supervisees may require work on transference with their supervisors and countertransference with their clients. Direct interventions for lower reactant supervisees involve clarifying the supervisory methods and addressing the miscommunications that occurred. Indirect interventions for higher reactance supervisees attend initially to their specific goals as opposed to immediately recognizing the underlying conflict. "Different strokes for different folks" works, even in handling conflicts in integrative supervision.

# 6

# Supervisor Development and Self-Care

These pages have been devoted so far to the development of supervisees and the care of their patients. In this chapter, we flip that focus and attend to the person and profession of the integrative supervisor. We address, in general order, the supervisor's ideal training, professional development, self-care and personal therapy, and continued learning. In all these topics, we draw attention to the distinctive features or twists of integrative supervisors.

## SUPERVISOR TRAINING

How would one ideally grow the integrative clinical supervisor? If we possessed the proverbial magic wand, then supervisors would be carefully developed and cultivated by a series of interlocking training experiences:

- admission into a competitive graduate program based on both academic qualifications and interpersonal qualities;

http://dx.doi.org/10.1037/15967-006
*Supervision Essentials for Integrative Psychotherapy*, by J. C. Norcross and L. M. Popple
Copyright © 2017 by the American Psychological Association. All rights reserved.

- several yearlong supervision experiences with competent, good-enough supervisors from several theoretical traditions;
- a strong supervisory alliance in two or more of those early supervision experiences, which models the methods and relationships as supervisees advance to the role of supervisor;
- sufficient breadth of clinical experience themselves, well beyond the required internship, working with diverse patients and in multiple clinical settings;
- a graduate course dedicated to clinical supervision, which would include experience in supervising other students (vertical supervision teams);
- concurrent or subsequent supervision of their early supervision activity;
- at least one successful episode of their own personal therapy;
- training in the core supervisory tasks shown to enhance supervision outcomes (as reviewed in the next chapter), including repairing ruptures (Safran, Muran, & Eubanks-Carter, 2011), managing countertransference (Ladany, Constantine, Miller, Erickson, & Muse-Burke, 2000), facilitating the supervisory alliance, monitoring patient improvement, and the like;
- competence in implementing the research on clinical supervision and on any clinical services they are supervising; and
- commitment to continued lifelong learning in clinical supervision (as described later).

## PROFESSIONAL DEVELOPMENT

The professional development of integrative supervisors seems to follow the trajectory of other supervisors: Read the supervision literature, attend conferences, participate in supervision research, and occasionally consult (and document the consultation) with fellow supervisors. In our home jurisdiction of Pennsylvania, licensed psychologists who supervise must complete a 3-hour continuing education course on supervision biennially.

We would add the requirement to share publicly your own clinical and supervision work in demonstrations, video recordings, and role plays. Supervisors, in our experience, delight in showcasing their shining moments in

their therapy cases; we prefer those who share their flummoxes and questionable interactions. That exposure, that vulnerability keeps supervisors more honest. An old joke holds that parenting and golfing keep adults humble. To that list, we would respectfully add showing one's own video recordings of unrehearsed sessions.

Every conference presentation on supervision—well, almost every one—brings us new realizations and skills. One of us (JCN) attended a workshop with the late Insoo Kim Berg (of solution-focused fame) and came away with a new appreciation for the language of "super-vision." That term can carry a pejorative, unintended sense of "superior" or "above," in contrast to a mutuality or peer-vision with advanced trainees and colleagues. In the solution-focused tradition, Berg taught linguistic methods to share power, let student cogenerate topics, adopt the supervisee perspective, teach curiosity, amplify success, and avoid the "should" and "must" whenever possible. The point is to capitalize on the clinical wisdom and research discoveries available to us throughout the professional life cycle.

In a virtuous cycle, doing supervision makes us better clinicians as well. We find each supervision hour affording in-depth moments to observe, process, discuss, and analyze clinical work, which yield a bounty of research and clinical insights.

One such moment of my (JCN) yearlong integrative supervision with LMP spurred a research study. In watching her termination work with clients, I wondered about her feelings of loss, which she immediately confirmed. I then asked how she had learned to express her loss to clients in ways that extended the work. LMP asked, "Do all therapists do that when saying goodbye?" Her inquiry propelled a recently completed study of 65 expert psychotherapists (of diverse theoretical orientations, of course) on their core termination behaviors. And yes, for the research record, 86% of expert therapists do acknowledge in session the bond and loss between the patient and themselves during termination (Norcross, Zimmerman, Greenberg, & Swift, 2016).

Every supervision experience yields something of value to one's continual development; even a stone can be a teacher (Kopp, 1985). Although I (LMP) have experienced less than favorable supervision in the past,

I honor it by learning how not to behave when I supervise others. I have learned not to be afraid to ask for what I need in supervision and to push myself outside my comfort zone with clients and in supervision.

All in all, conducting supervision emerges as one of the most rewarding professional activities—a constant source of learning, engagement, and surprise. Many of the manifest gratifications of supervision were summarized decades ago by Ekstein and Wallerstein (1972): offering real choices to students on the road toward mature professional self-realization; helping independent minds to flourish and challenge; discovering that some supervisees may later be friends and scientific coworkers; developing methods that ensure growth in knowledge and skill; guaranteeing collaborators who stimulate us to test and refine those methods; assisting supervisees in identifying with the noble activity of supervision; facilitating supervisees' own process of growth; and becoming an eternal learner. Not a bad gig, that.

## SELF-CARE AND PERSONAL THERAPY

These two topics strike at the heart of developing psychotherapists, and each deserves book-length consideration. Fortunately, one of us (JCN) has already coauthored books on self-care (Norcross & Guy, 2007) and personal therapy (Geller, Norcross, & Orlinsky, 2005). But please do not expect extended consideration of them here, as integrative supervisors fall for the most part into the mainstream of their other-theory-minded colleagues.

### Self-Care

Psychotherapists, by definition, study and modify human behavior; that is, we study and modify other humans. Psychological principles and methods are rarely brought to bear on ourselves (with the probable exception of our unsolicited attempts to diagnose one another). Integrative supervisors, like other competent supervisors, understand this dearth of training attention to self-care and try to remediate it accordingly.

Part of that effort, as illustrated in the companion DVD, is to inquire on occasion about supervisee self-care. We periodically raise the issue of self-care, particularly when prompted by stressful clinical interactions and unsettling life events. Sometimes raising the topic is enough for supervisees, and other times a more elaborate intervention is needed to ensure they are taking care of themselves. Likewise, modeling self-care as a supervisor assists supervisees in recognizing the ethical imperative and professional responsibility of tending to oneself while tending to others. Through discussion, modeling, reading, and assessments, we prize self-care of the supervisee and supervisors.

Just as being a lawyer does not make one more honest and being a physician does not make one healthier, being a psychotherapist does not make one automatically more proficient at self-care. In fact, the converse is frequently true.

The self-care of integrative practitioners (and presumably, supervisors) tends to diverge from others in going broader rather than deeper (Norcross, 2000). Compared with their psychodynamic, cognitive–behavioral, and humanistic colleagues, integrative therapists consistently report employing more self-care strategies. They become more pragmatic, eclectic, and "secular" in their own self-care when confronting distress. They seem to recognize that the effect of any single strategy is rather modest; possessing a particular skill in one's arsenal is less consequential than having a variety of self-care strategies. Perhaps integrative therapists have extended valuable lessons from their clinical work to their personal lives: Avoid concentration on a single theory and promote cognitive and experiential growth on a broad front; that is, embrace multiple strategies associated with diverse theoretical traditions.

And those self-care strategies do emerge from assorted traditions, inside and outside of psychology proper. Our thumbnail synopsis encompasses the following 12 self-care strategies (Norcross & Guy, 2007):

1. Value the person of the psychotherapist.
2. Refocus on the rewards.
3. Recognize the hazards.
4. Mind the body.

5. Nurture relationships.
6. Set boundaries.
7. Restructure cognitions.
8. Sustain healthy escapes.
9. Create a flourishing environment.
10. Undergo personal therapy.
11. Cultivate spirituality and mission.
12. Foster creativity and growth.

## Personal Therapy

That 10th self-care principle—undergo personal therapy—has been a topic of keen interest to the profession and to us for decades (Norcross, 2005). The interest originated not only in my personal therapy but also from the anecdotal discoveries of one of my early mentors (Lazarus, 1971) that the majority of behavior therapists were not selecting behavior therapy for themselves. Five of our subsequent studies determined an identical pattern: The vast majority of behavior therapists choose nonbehavioral personal therapy. Psychotherapists value clinical strategies quite different from what they offer their clients or from what they consider to be within their competence. On a personal, if not a professional, level, clinicians take psychotherapy integration to heart.

We (but not all integrative supervisors) place personal therapy at the epicenter of psychotherapy training. It forms, along with working with patients and in supervision, the deepest and most rigorous part of one's clinical education. In *Analysis Terminable and Interminable*, Freud (1937/1964) asked, "But where and how is the poor wretch to acquire the ideal qualification which he will need in this profession? The answer is in an analysis of himself, with which his preparation for his future activity begins" (p. 246). In one of our studies (Norcross, Dryden, & DeMichele, 1992), only 4% of psychologists who received personal therapy thought it was unimportant as a prerequisite for conducting clinical work compared with 39% of those psychologists who had not undergone personal therapy. Our training, identity, health, and self-renewal revolve around personal therapy.

The vast majority of mental health professionals have undergone personal treatment. In a review of 17 studies involving more than 8,000 mental health professionals, approximately 75% had received at least one episode of personal therapy themselves (Norcross & Guy, 2005). The prevalence of personal therapy varies systematically with theoretical orientation. Psychoanalytic clinicians have the highest rates (82% to 100%) and behavior therapists the lowest (44% to 66%), with integrative/eclectic therapists toward the higher end.

A pernicious myth persists that most mental health professionals do not experience the need for personal therapy once they are in practice; however, the evidence rebuts any such illusion. Most seasoned clinicians (range = 43%–62%) do in fact utilize the very services they provide. Psychotherapists seeking personal treatment repeatedly during their careers supports the conclusion that such treatment is widely perceived not only as an essential part of the formative training phase but also as an important component in the practitioner's ongoing maturation and regenerative development.

There is no controlled research attesting that receipt of personal therapy is positively or negatively related to client outcome. Because all studies on this matter have suffered from the absence of large samples, controls, random assignment to personal therapy or nontherapy, and prospective designs, the vital data necessarily come from psychotherapist research. There the evidence for supervisor development is indirect but plentiful on (a) enhanced relational skills, (b) improved personal functioning, and (c) enriched professional development (see Norcross, 2005; Orlinsky & Norcross, 2005).

The primary goal of the psychotherapist's personal treatment is indeed personal; that is, to enhance the awareness, functioning, and life satisfaction of the person who, coincidentally, is a mental health professional. A secondary goal of personal treatment is to alter the nature of subsequent therapeutic work in ways that enhance its effectiveness. Personal treatment is designed both to enhance the personal functioning of the person and to improve his or her professional performance (Geller, Norcross, & Orlinsky, 2005).

The mechanisms of securing these twin goals are as complex and individualized as the number of therapist–patients. Nonetheless, there are at

least six recurring commonalities in the literature on how the therapist's therapy is said to improve his or her clinical work. Personal treatment

- improves the emotional and mental functioning of the psychotherapist: It makes the clinician's life less neurotic and more gratifying in a profession where one's personal health is an indispensable foundation.
- provides the therapist–patient with a more complete understanding of personal dynamics, interpersonal elicitations, and internal conflicts: The therapist can thereby conduct treatment with clearer perception, less contaminated reactions, and reduced countertransference potential.
- alleviates the emotional stresses and burdens inherent in the practice of psychotherapy: It enables practitioners to deal more successfully with the special problems imposed by the craft.
- serves as a profound socialization experience: It establishes a sense of conviction about the validity of psychotherapy, demonstrates its transformational power in their own lives, and facilitates the internalization of the healer role.
- places therapists in the role of the client: It thus sensitizes them to the interpersonal reactions and needs of their clients and increases respect for their patients' struggles.
- provides a firsthand, intensive opportunity to observe clinical methods: The therapist's therapist models interpersonal and technical skills.

For all these reasons, we strongly encourage personal therapy as part of clinical training and supervisor development.

## Personal Development Activities

Although convinced of the extraordinary power and socialization of personal therapy, we are reluctant to require a single growth experience of uniform length for diverse students. Such a requirement would probably violate the integrative maxim of "different strokes for different folks." Instead, we endorse broader, more flexible opportunities for personal development and life-improving activities. This would certainly include personal therapy but also retreats, support groups, self-help activities, meditation, development

exercises, process groups, and other means of enhancement and experimentation. Grow the supervisee by all effective means available.

## ONGOING LEARNING AND CONSULTATION

As a matter of professional development and ethical behavior, integrative supervisors make a lifetime commitment to competence. What better vehicle than continual lifelong education? *CE* becomes shorthand for "craving education" rather than the dreaded obligatory "continuing education."

Deliberate practice makes the integrative master. Consistent with the research on expert performance, the amount of time spent in improving therapeutic skills significantly predicts client outcomes (e.g., Chow et al., 2015; Persons, Hong, Eidelman, & Owen, 2016). We extrapolate this body of therapy research to supervision: The amount of time devoted to improving supervision skills probably enhances supervisee outcomes as well. Self-reflection and self-practice may entail reviewing recordings of supervision sessions, using self-reflection sheets, collecting independent feedback on performance, undergoing supervision of our own supervision, and seeking consultation. Multiple methods will probably lead to the most practice improvement.

Over the past decade, I (JCN) have been increasingly approached by seasoned colleagues to provide supervision of their supervision and have done so on multiple occasions. (In truth, I prefer the terms *peer-vision* or *consultation* in these instances.) The paradox: Those colleagues keenly seeking such supervision prove, nine times out of 10, to be the most skilled supervisors; those disinterested or seeking it only under duress turn out to usually be the worst. Practice may make perfect, but dedication to excellence also factors into the equation.

Finally, ongoing education brings continual challenge and joy. Each time we experiment with a new client feedback system, learn a recent therapy method, or implement a supervision process written up in a journal, we become energized and refreshed. A supervisee once pointed at my huge reading pile of journals, books, and DVDs and innocently asked: "Does it ever stop?" I (JCN) replied, "I certainly hope not!" and then invoked the Yiddish proverb, "The sea has no shore; learning has no end."

# Research Support

As with psychotherapy itself, it is increasingly difficult to speak of psychotherapy supervision without reference to its demonstrated efficacy. The introduction of an integrative perspective does nothing to reduce the challenge of researching the subtle and complex effects of supervision on trainees and their clients. Indeed, integration probably enlarges the task of measuring supervision outcomes.

Research support for integrative supervision comes in two broad guises: research on what works in general for clinical supervision, and research on what works in particular for integrative supervision. Following are a few paragraphs on what we know in general and then more elaborate discussion on exciting but preliminary controlled research on the comparative effectiveness of integrative supervision.

---

http://dx.doi.org/10.1037/15967-007
*Supervision Essentials for Integrative Psychotherapy*, by J. C. Norcross and L. M. Popple
Copyright © 2017 by the American Psychological Association. All rights reserved.

## WHAT WE KNOW IN GENERAL FROM THE SUPERVISION RESEARCH

First and most generally, the entire body of supervision research informs integrative supervision. A genuine advantage of being integrative involves the ability to harvest the extant research on supervision and cull what works for all supervisees and then among different supervisees. Integration tries to incorporate state-of-the-art research findings into its open, evolving system.

Researchers have been investigating and debating the effectiveness of clinical supervision for decades (M. V. Ellis & Ladany, 1997; Lambert & Ogles, 1997). In truth, we do not possess sufficient quantity or quality of randomized controlled trials to address the question of whether supervision substantially improves the treatment outcomes of the supervisee. The extant research has largely addressed the effects of supervision not on patient benefit but on satisfaction with supervision, the supervisory alliance, and supervisee self-ratings (Freitas, 2002; Milne, Aylott, Fitzpatrick, & Ellis, 2008). In attempting to bridge the science and practice of clinical supervision across 28 years of research, M. V. Ellis (2010) conceded that "it is a bridge under construction" (p. 110).

What we have from the large body of less than methodologically rigorous research is a finite list of good practices or evidence-based principles on conducting supervision. The hundreds of research reports, as distilled by numerous reviewers (e.g., American Psychological Association, 2015; Bernard & Goodyear, 2014; M. V. Ellis, 2010; M. V. Ellis & Ladany, 1997; Milne et al., 2008), boil down to the following:

- cultivating a warm, trusting supervisory alliance;
- attending to alliance ruptures and managing countertransference;
- using an informed consent and written contract (goal setting);
- observing what supervisees actually do in session;
- focusing on supervisee competencies and attaining minimal levels of those competencies;
- providing plentiful formative feedback and occasional summative feedback;
- modeling or demonstrating skills to be learned;
- teaching technical, relational, and conceptual skills to supervisees;

- monitoring the progress of supervisees' patients;
- maintaining proper boundaries and modeling ethical conduct;
- documenting what transpires in supervision (and any deficits in the relationship and in supervisees);
- attending to the cultural identities of all participants in the supervisory triad (patient, supervisee, supervisor); and
- individualizing/personalizing supervision to the singular supervisee and particular context.

Of particular import is the fact that none of these research-supported principles or evidence-based practices hail from a single theoretical tradition. None are restricted to a single theoretical model. We embrace these robust common factors and, at the same time, capitalize on the key differences among supervisees. Call us biased, but we characterize the cumulative results of the research as unequivocally supporting integrative supervision!

## WHAT WE KNOW IN PARTICULAR FROM THE INTEGRATIVE RESEARCH

Second, and specific to integrative supervision, is the research investigating its success. In previous chapters, we have outlined the extensive body of research that supports integrative psychotherapy, not supervision per se; that is, we have reviewed the multiple meta-analyses demonstrating that adapting or personalizing psychotherapy to patient transdiagnostic features (stages, preferences, reactance, culture, and the like) improves treatment outcome and decreases dropouts. That research evidence is strong and compelling, but what has not been empirically compelling is whether integrative psychotherapy can be learned through integrative supervision and, thereby, produce increased benefit for patients.

To be sure, decades of integrative supervision conducted by colleagues and me (JCN) support increased patient benefit. Hundreds of supervisees have discovered more efficacious and efficient therapy as a result of a systematic integrative way of working. But most supervisors would make similar claims. Can we demonstrate in controlled research that integrative supervision produces superior therapy outcomes for our supervisees' patients?

A recent study addressed this question directly for one form of integrative supervision: Systematic Treatment Selection (STS; Beutler, Clarkin, & Bongar, 2000; Norcross & Beutler, 2014). The controlled study used a matched clinical trial design with quasi-random assignment of therapists to supervisors and a rotation schedule of assigning patients to therapists (Holt et al., 2015). The therapists were doctoral students in clinical psychology, with at least 2 years of clinical experience. They received supervision as usual (SAU) or supervision by STS-trained supervisors (SAS). The outcome analysis was based on a matched 2 (SAS vs. SAU) × 3 (time) using pre–post administrations of the Outcome Questionnaire-45 (OQ-45).

Supervisors who volunteered to participate in the study were first trained in STS supervision. The matching principles were those that had earned particularly strong outcome effect sizes in meta-analytic reviews of extant literature (Castonguay & Beutler, 2017; Norcross, 2011) as reviewed earlier in these pages, such as adapting therapy to patient reactance level, coping style, preferences, and stages of change. The training program outlined session-by-session tasks for each supervisor to use with the participating PhD and PsyD supervisees, for either eight-session or 16-session treatments. Supervision included a presentation of each matching principle in sequence, a discussion of how to implement it, and a periodic in-session rating of compliance of the student's interventions with STS.

Supervision was supplemented by the use of the InnerLife STS, a cloud-based assessment of the patient problem areas, STS patient characteristics, and treatment recommendations based on the STS principles. InnerLife also provided several graphic representations of intake symptoms, risk, and treatment planning variables that were used in supervision.

Patients in the study were sequential admissions to a university outpatient clinic. Their diagnoses varied, reflecting the nature and location of the clinic. Principal diagnoses included depressive, anxiety, and personality disorders, averaging within the moderate range of severity. Routinely, the clinic referred out those patients with active psychoses and those for whom long-term treatment was indicated. Socioeconomic characteristics of the patients tended toward low income and marginal employment, not atypical of other sliding-fee clinics.

Each patient who received SAS was matched both with the next patient who entered treatment in the clinic and with the one who immediately preceded the SAS patient. SAS and SAU patients did not differ by demographics or diagnoses. At the end of treatment, the patients seen in both types of supervision were compared on standard outcome measures, including the OQ-45.

Student therapists who received the integrative STS supervision produced enhanced outcomes over those achieved by students receiving supervision as usual. At the end of treatment (averaged across treatment length) the pre–post effect size ($d$) of patients seeing SAU trainees was a respectable 0.72. However, the effect size achieved by the SAS group was substantially larger ($d = 1.37$), with 81% of the patients in this group returning to "normal" functioning based on final outcome scores. The added contributions of STS supervision over regular supervision can be described as an effect ($d$) of 0.65. Thus, in a community setting with diverse patients, STS supervision produced increased patient benefit over typical supervision (Stein et al., 2016). Both a supervisor effect and a time-in-treatment effect were ruled out as contributing to the differences noted. The only reliable predictor of outcome was type of supervision (SAS vs. SAU).

These impressive results from a single setting require replication, of course. At the same time, preliminary results parallel the increased psychotherapy benefits found for fitting therapy to the patient, as reviewed in Chapter 2 (this volume). To our knowledge, this is one of the first controlled studies to show differential patient improvement for trainees receiving a particular form of supervision—integrative supervision.

In sum, integrative supervisors commit to evidence-based practice: leveraging the best available research, building on clinician expertise, and incorporating patient/supervisee values, preferences, and characteristics. The available research supporting integrative supervision emanates from both the large general body of supervision literature and the nascent specific body of controlled outcome research. As the field of psychotherapy inexorably evolves toward integration, we eagerly anticipate the production of more research that will sharpen and enhance clinical supervision.

# 8

# Conclusions and Future Directions

Mental health professionals have been traditionally taught in either the isolated single-theory approach or the multiple competing-theory approach. The single-theory concentration suggests that "this" is the one and only truth, whereas the multitheory comparison suggests that no truth exists. The result is frequently the production of either narrow adherents to orthodoxy or broadly based practitioners who possess a confused hodgepodge of partial competencies. We immodestly insist that there is a better way—systematic, research-informed integration—and it is available now for training and supervision.

In just the past 2 decades, integrative supervision has morphed in clinical sophistication and research support. When I (JCN) began my graduate training in 1980, "eclectic" supervision was prototypically performed from the supervisor's idiosyncratic and unarticulated perspective. Laudable "what works," seat-of-the-pants eclecticism and "each client is

http://dx.doi.org/10.1037/15967-008
*Supervision Essentials for Integrative Psychotherapy*, by J. C. Norcross and L. M. Popple
Copyright © 2017 by the American Psychological Association. All rights reserved.

different" pluralism reigned, but without specific direction or supporting research. In the future, integrative supervision will be guided by a systematic process and an empirical frame. It's not your parent's fuzzy eclecticism anymore.

In the past, too, integrative supervision was largely concerned with the selection of a clinical technique for a particular problem—what we characterize as method X for disorder Z. In the present and future, integrative supervision assists trainees in selecting not only the "treatments of choice" but also the "therapeutic relationships of choice" for diagnostic and especially transdiagnostic features of the client. This adaptation or responsiveness in psychotherapy and in supervision closely resembles precision or personalized medicine: determining how each individual can heal and grow best.

We have every reason to believe in a positive future for integrative supervision. Integration, in its multiple guides, continues as the modal orientation of mental health professionals. The cumulative research on effective supervision, as reviewed in Chapter 7 of this book, certainly supports transtheoretical supervision. The confluence of competency-focused education and evidence-based practice favors integration, as does the migration of clinical services to other health care settings where interdisciplinarity and globality hold sway. Insurance carriers and more patients insist on personalized and research-supported treatments in the integrative tradition. Psychotherapy experts forecast escalating popularity of integration well into the 21st century (Norcross, Pfund, & Prochaska, 2013).

Research demonstrates that the vast majority of psychology, psychiatry, counseling, and social work training programs profess a pro-integration position (e.g., D. M. Allen, Kennedy, Veeser, & Grosso, 2000; Goldner-deBeer, 1999; Lampropoulos & Dixon, 2007). Training directors report that they are committed to providing their students with significant exposure to the major psychotherapy models and to encouraging their students to seek out practica that expose them to different treatment approaches. And, in most training programs, the attitudes of students are positive toward integration as well.

What might the future of integrative supervision portend? We confidently predict four directions: competency benchmarks, technological advances, individual and cultural differences, and outcome research.

CONCLUSIONS AND FUTURE DIRECTIONS

## COMPETENCY BENCHMARKS

The competence of our graduates and, indeed, the adequacy of our supervision have been typically assumed rather than verified. For more than 50 years neither supervisees nor supervisors have needed to actually demonstrate their competence (Kaslow, 2004). Most psychotherapy supervisors have not received formal training or supervision themselves in the activity. In the future, integrative supervisors will be expected to complete a formal course in supervision, will be supervised in supervision, and will be held to a higher standard of performance. Not a moment too soon! Fully half of psychotherapy supervisees across professions report harmful supervision at some point in their training and fully three quarters experience inadequate supervision at some point (M. V. Ellis, 2010).

Supervision itself will increasingly be recognized as a core competency of mental health professionals. Competency requirements, now standard fare in other health professions, will be here soon and represent a transformational moment (Kaslow, Falender, & Grus, 2012). Multiple guidelines for supervisors (e.g., American Psychological Association, 2015) and competency benchmarks (e.g., Fouad et al., 2009) are already available. Competency in clinical supervision has finally come of age.

One of our favorite cartoons shows, in a single panel, a man walking out to an automobile and throwing the car keys to someone else while quipping: "You drive. I'll criticize!" That cartoon aptly describes part of psychotherapy, and if we're honest, part of clinical supervision. It is so, so much easier to criticize someone else's behavior than to risk exposure and vulnerability one's self. But we predict greater availability of more video recordings and demonstrations of integrative supervision in the quest to provide public examples of competent supervision.

## TECHNOLOGICAL ADVANCES

We are approaching the tipping point for technology in integrative supervision. Virtual therapies and distance supervision—with their attendant legal, ethical, and regulatory tangles—are here to stay.

The complexity of psychotherapy spirals as we realize the ways that multiple diagnostic and transdiagnostic variables interact with one another. Computer technologies possess the potential to provide effective assessment and to assist clinicians in customizing treatments in the face of an endless variety of permutating patient qualities. Humans can fluidly process only four variables simultaneously (Halford, Baker, McCredden, & Bain, 2005), but computers can efficiently take on more permutations.

InnerLife Systematic Treatment Selection (STS) is a cloud-based assessment and monitoring app for psychotherapy patients. As described in Chapter 7, it assesses multiple transdiagnostic patient features, symptom presentations, and complexity and then offers evidence-based treatment and self-help guidelines based on algorithms. (Disclaimer: I [JCN] am a research scientist for InnerLife STS.) Such technologies will make multiple identifications of treatment adaptations easier and in a more reliable way for integrative supervisees and supervisors in the future.

In that STS tradition (Beutler & Harwood, 2004), virtual reality technology has been applied to training psychotherapists. Visual renditions of patients who represent predefined characteristics—say, the precontemplation stage of change or low reactance—help supervisees learn to recognize indicating and contraindicating cues while also offering immediate feedback, in the form of patient response, about the appropriateness of the selected treatments. These procedures are designed to assist supervisees in identifying patient behaviors and cues that invoke the use of different relational stances and treatment strategies. Such methodology may improve training, all in the safety of a "virtual" therapeutic environment.

## INDIVIDUAL AND CULTURAL DIFFERENCES

The mental health professions have properly begun attending to the various *isms*—racism, sexism, heterosexism, ageism, and others—that have damaged our society, health care, and clinical training. In the future, we foresee these individual and cultural differences serving not as roadblocks but as vehicles for improving the effectiveness and applicability of psychotherapy.

A foundational lesson mastered by every Psych 101 student is that people differ. These human differences translate into potent transdiagnostic adaptations that improve clinical services. Racial/ethnic adaptations of psychological and medical treatments enhance care and reduce health disparities for people of color; religious/spiritual adaptations of psychological treatments increase retention and promote spirituality among people of faith; relational adaptations for clients responding better to more or less therapist directiveness produce better outcomes; and preference adaptations for clients seeking pharmacotherapy, psychotherapy, and/or self-help make for better fits and better utilization of resources. Our treasured differences become a source of strength and guidance in integrative supervision.

## OUTCOME RESEARCH

We seek to conduct integrative supervision in which the supervisee feels trusted and respected, in which he or she grows and develops as a professional. These laudable criteria will be complemented increasingly in the future by the more urgent ethical standard of patient benefit. Did the patients treated by the integrative supervisee prosper? We think of this as our ethical duty, our "prime directive" (as characterized on *Star Trek*). Inside and outside the profession, we are forcibly reminded that the ultimate objective of supervision is to improve treatment outcomes. Protecting the public and enhancing health are the ultimate responsibilities of clinical supervision.

As is true for every genre of clinical supervision, the future will bring more published research on the outcomes of integrative supervision. The impressive early results on the differential success of integrative supervision (see Chapter 7) require replication across settings and investigators. Does the promise of added patient benefit stand the test of time?

As well, we require more research on tailoring or customizing supervision to the individual trainee. The current models are noble but obviously incomplete. Which supervisee dimensions identified in Chapter 3—supervisee preferences, developmental stage, therapy approach, cognitive

style/reactance level, cultural identities, and clinical setting—prove essential for such tailoring? Or perhaps the beneficial effect resides largely in the relational aspect of trying to personalize the supervision, not so much in the actual method? All these models await research explication and validation in the next decade.

In the meantime, we work integratively in supervision with the assurance that history demonstrates integration is the inevitable route of the sciences and the professions (Feyerabend, 1970; Kuhn, 1970). Clinical supervision, following the field of psychotherapy, is experiencing both a decline in ideological struggle and a movement toward rapprochement. The convergence of science and practice in supervision—if still a bridge under construction (M. V. Ellis, 2010)—favors the integrative path. We envision a future in which supervisors deliver integrative processes and products that are less parochial, more pluralistic, and more effective than traditional, single theories. In that future, effective supervision will be defined, not by its brand or school name, but by how well it grows supervisees and improves patient care.

# Suggested Readings

American Psychological Association. (2015). Guidelines for clinical supervision in health service psychology. *American Psychologist, 70,* 33–46.

APA's supervision guidelines are among the most recent and comprehensive of the genre; a blend of best practices, research evidence, and preachy exhortation.

Bernard, J. M., & Goodyear, R. K. (2014). *Fundamentals of clinical supervision* (5th ed.). New York, NY: Pearson.

It features a splendid integration of research findings and supervision measures.

Norcross, J. C. (2011). (Ed.). *Psychotherapy relationships that work* (2nd ed.). New York, NY: Oxford University Press.

A summary of meta-analytic results and clinical practices on effective elements of the therapeutic relationship (what works in general) and on effective methods to tailor therapy to the individual (what works in particular).

Norcross, J. C. (2013). *Integrative therapy* [DVD]. Washington, DC: American Psychological Association.

A videotaped illustration and discussion of integrative therapy that emphasizes tailoring to the individual client; here's how one of the authors does it.

Norcross, J. C., & Goldfried, M. R. (Eds.). (2005). *Handbook of psychotherapy integration* (2nd ed.). New York, NY: Oxford University Press.

A comprehensive overview of the history, practice, training, research, and contributions of psychotherapy integration.

Norcross, J. C., & Guy, J. D. (Eds.). (2007). *Leaving it at the office: A guide to psychotherapist self-care.* New York, NY: Guilford.

A primer on necessary self-care for mental health professionals.

Prochaska, J. O., & Norcross, J. C. (2013). *Systems of psychotherapy: A transtheoretical analysis* (8th ed.). Pacific Grove, CA: Cengage-Brooks/Cole.

A thorough description and comparative analysis of the leading theories/systems of psychotherapy; one cannot integrate what one does not know.

# References

Allen, D. M., Kennedy, C. L., Veeser, W. R., & Grosso, T. (2000). Teaching the integration of psychotherapy paradigms in a psychiatric residency seminar. *Academic Psychiatry, 24*, 6–13. http://dx.doi.org/10.1007/BF03340066

Allen, G. J., Szollos, S. J., & Williams, B. E. (1986). Doctoral students' comparative evaluations of best and worst psychotherapy supervision. *Professional Psychology: Research and Practice, 17*, 91–99. http://dx.doi.org/10.1037/0735-7028.17.2.91

Allison, K. W., Crawford, I., Echemendia, R., Robinson, L., & Knepp, D. (1994). Human diversity and professional competence: Training in clinical and counseling psychology revisited. *American Psychologist, 49*, 792–796. http://dx.doi.org/10.1037/0003-066X.49.9.792

American Psychological Association. (2015). Guidelines for clinical supervision in health service psychology. *American Psychologist, 70*, 33–46. http://dx.doi.org/10.1037/a0038112

Andrews, J. D. W., Norcross, J. C., & Halgin, R. P. (1992). Training in psychotherapy integration. In J. C. Norcross & M. R. Goldfried (Eds.), *Handbook of psychotherapy integration* (pp. 563–591). New York, NY: Basic Books.

Arkowitz, S. W. (2001). Perfectionism in the supervisee. In S. Gill (Ed.), *The supervisory alliance: Facilitating the psychotherapist's learning experience*. Northvale, NJ: Jason Aronson.

Austad, C. S., Sherman, W. O., Morgan, T., & Holstein, L. (1992). The psychotherapist and the managed care setting. *Professional Psychology: Research and Practice, 23*, 329–332.

Berger, S. S., & Buchholz, E. S. (1993). On becoming a supervisee: Preparation for learning in a supervisory relationship. *Psychotherapy: Theory, Research, Practice, Training, 30*, 86–92. http://dx.doi.org/10.1037/0033-3204.30.1.86

# REFERENCES

Bernal, G., & Rodriguez, M. M. D. (Eds.). (2012). *Cultural adaptations: Tools for evidence-based practice with diverse populations.* Washington, DC: American Psychological Association. http://dx.doi.org/10.1037/13752-000

Bernard, J. M., & Goodyear, R. K. (2014). *Fundamentals of clinical supervision* (5th ed.). New York, NY: Pearson.

Beutler, L. E. (1999). Manualizing flexibility: The training of eclectic therapists. *Journal of Clinical Psychology, 55,* 399–404. http://dx.doi.org/10.1002/(SICI)1097-4679(199904)55:4<399::AID-JCLP4>3.0.CO;2-Z

Beutler, L. E., & Clarkin, J. (1990). *Systematic treatment selection: Toward targeted therapeutic interventions.* New York, NY: Brunner/Mazel.

Beutler, L. E., Clarkin, J., & Bongar, B. (2000). *Guidelines for the systematic treatment of the depressed patient.* New York, NY: Oxford University Press. http://dx.doi.org/10.1093/acprof:oso/9780195105308.001.0001

Beutler, L. E., & Harwood, T. M. (2000). *Prescriptive psychotherapy: A practical guide to systematic treatment selection.* New York, NY: Oxford University Press. http://dx.doi.org/10.1093/med:psych/9780195136692.001.0001

Beutler, L. E., & Harwood, T. M. (2004). Virtual reality in psychotherapy training. *Journal of Clinical Psychology, 60,* 317–330. http://dx.doi.org/10.1002/jclp.10266

Beutler, L. E., Harwood, T. M., Michelson, A., Song, X., & Holman, J. (2011). Reactance/resistance. In J. C. Norcross (Ed.), *Psychotherapy relationships that work* (2nd ed., pp. 261–278). New York, NY: Oxford University Press.

Beutler, L. E., Mahoney, M. J., Norcross, J. C., Prochaska, J. O., Sollod, R. M., & Robertson, M. (1987). Training integrative and eclectic psychotherapists II. *Journal of Integrative & Eclectic Psychotherapy, 6,* 296–332.

Bordin, E. S. (1983). A working alliance model of supervision. *The Counseling Psychologist, 11,* 35–42. http://dx.doi.org/10.1177/0011000083111007

Bucky, S. T., Marques, S., Daly, J., Alley, J., & Karp, A. (2010). Supervision characteristics related to the supervisory working alliance as rated by doctoral-level supervisees. *The Clinical Supervisor, 29,* 149–163. http://dx.doi.org/10.1080/07325223.2010.519270

Burkard, A. W., Johnson, A. J., Madson, M. B., Pruitt, N. T., Contreras-Tadych, D. A., Kozlowski, J. M., . . . Knox, S. (2006). Supervisor cultural responsiveness and unresponsiveness in cross-cultural supervision. *Journal of Counseling Psychology, 53,* 288–301. http://dx.doi.org/10.1037/0022-0167.53.3.288

Burlingame, G., McClendon, D. T., & Alonso, J. (2011). Group cohesion. In J. C. Norcross (Ed.), *Psychotherapy relationships that work* (2nd ed., pp. 110–131). New York, NY: Oxford University Press. http://dx.doi.org/10.1093/acprof:oso/9780199737208.003.0005

# REFERENCES

Carifio, M. S., & Hess, A. K. (1987). Who is the ideal supervisor? *Professional Psychology: Research and Practice, 18*, 244–250. http://dx.doi.org/10.1037/0735-7028.18.3.244

Castonguay, L. G. (2000). A common factors approach to psychotherapy training. *Journal of Psychotherapy Integration, 10*, 263–282. http://dx.doi.org/10.1023/A:1009496929012

Castonguay, L. G., & Beutler, L. E. (Eds.). (2017). *Principles of therapeutic change that work* (Vol. 2). New York, NY: Oxford University Press.

Castonguay, L. G., Schut, A. J., Aikins, D. E., Constantino, M. J., Laurenceau, J. P., Bologh, L., & Burns, D. D. (2004). Integrative cognitive therapy for depression: A preliminary investigation. *Journal of Psychotherapy Integration, 14*, 4–20.

Chopra, T. (2013). All supervision is multicultural: A review of literature on the need for multicultural supervision in counseling. *Psychological Studies, 58*, 335–338. http://dx.doi.org/10.1007/s12646-013-0206-x

Chow, D. L., Miller, S. D., Seidel, J. A., Kane, R. T., Thornton, J. A., & Andrews, W. P. (2015). The role of deliberate practice in the development of highly effective psychotherapists. *Psychotherapy, 52*, 337–345. http://dx.doi.org/10.1037/pst0000015

Constantine, M. G., Ladany, N., Inman, A. G., & Ponterotto, J. G. (1996). Students' perceptions of multicultural training in counseling psychology programs. *Journal of Multicultural Counseling and Development, 24*, 241–253. http://dx.doi.org/10.1002/j.2161-1912.1996.tb00306.x

Cook, J. M., Biyanova, T., Elhai, J., Schnurr, P. P., & Coyne, J. C. (2010). What do psychotherapists really do in practice? An internet study of over 2,000 practitioners. *Psychotherapy, 47*, 260–267.

Demorest, A. P. (2004). *Psychology's grand theorists: How personal experiences shaped professional ideas.* Mahwah, NJ: Erlbaum.

Dryden, W., & Spurling, L. (Eds.). (1989). *On becoming a psychotherapist.* London, England: Tavistock/Routledge.

Duncan, B. L., Miller, S. D., Sparks, J. A., Claud, D. A., Reynolds, L. R., Brown, J., & Johnson, L. D. (2003). The session rating scale: Preliminary psychometric properties of a working alliance measure. *Journal of Brief Therapy, 3*, 3–12.

Ekstein, R., & Wallerstein, R. S. (1972). *The teaching and learning of psychotherapy* (Rev. ed.). Oxford, England: International Universities Press.

Elliott, R., Bohart, A. C., Watson, J. C., & Greenberg, L. S. (2011). Empathy. In J. C. Norcross (Ed.), *Psychotherapy relationships that work* (2nd ed., pp. 132–152). New York, NY: Oxford University Press. http://dx.doi.org/10.1093/acprof:oso/9780199737208.003.0006

Ellis, M. V. (2006). Critical incidents in clinical supervision and in supervisor supervision: Assessing supervisory issues. *Training and Education in Professional Psychology, S*(2), 122–132. http://dx.doi.org/10.1037/1931-3918.S.2.122

Ellis, M. V. (2010). Bridging the science and practice of clinical supervision: Some discoveries, some misconceptions. *The Clinical Supervisor, 29*, 95–116. http://dx.doi.org/10.1080/07325221003741910

Ellis, M. V., & Ladany, N. (1997). Inferences concerning supervisees and clients in clinical supervision: An integrative review. In C. E. Watkins, Jr. (Ed.), *Handbook of psychotherapy supervision* (pp. 447–507). Hoboken, NJ: Wiley.

Ellis, S., Carette, B., Anseel, F., & Lievens, F. (2014). Systematic reflection: Implications for learning from failures and successes. *Current Directions in Psychological Science, 23*, 67–72. http://dx.doi.org/10.1177/0963721413504106

Falender, C. A., & Shafranske, E. P. (2011). *Getting the most out of clinical training and supervision: A guide for practicum students and interns*. Washington, DC: American Psychological Association.

Farber, B. (2006). Supervisee and supervisor disclosure. In B. Farber (Ed.), *Self-disclosure in psychotherapy* (pp. 180–197). New York, NY: Guilford Press.

Farber, B. A., & Doolin, E. M. (2011). Positive regard. In J. C. Norcross (Ed.), *Psychotherapy relationships that work* (2nd ed., pp. 168–186). New York, NY: Oxford University Press. http://dx.doi.org/10.1093/acprof:oso/9780199737208.003.0008

Feyerabend, P. (1970). Consolations for the specialist. In I. Lakatos & A. E. Musgrave (Eds.), *Criticism and the growth of knowledge* (pp. 59–89). Cambridge, England: Cambridge University.

Fiscalini, J. (1985). On supervisory parataxis and dialogue. *Contemporary Psychoanalysis, 21*, 591–608.

Fouad, N. A., Grus, C. L., Hatcher, R. L., Kaslow, N. J., Hutchings, P. S., Madson, M. B., . . . Crossman, R. E. (2009). Competency benchmarks: A model for understanding and measuring competence in professional psychology across training levels. *Training and Education in Professional Psychology, 3*(Suppl.), S5–S26. http://dx.doi.org/10.1037/a0015832

Frances, A., & Clarkin, J. F. (1981). Parallel techniques in supervision and treatment. *Psychiatric Quarterly, 53*, 242–248. http://dx.doi.org/10.1007/BF01070098

Frank, J. D. (1973). *Persuasion and healing* (2nd ed.). Baltimore, MD: Johns Hopkins University.

Freitas, G. J. (2002). The impact of psychotherapy supervision on client outcome: A critical examination of 2 decades of research. *Psychotherapy: Theory, Research, Practice, Training, 39*, 354–367.

French, T. M. (1933). Interrelations between psychoanalysis and the experimental work of Pavlov. *American Journal of Psychiatry, 89*, 1165–1203.

Freud, S. (1964). Analysis terminable and interminable. In J. Strachey (Ed. and Trans.), *The standard edition of the complete psychological works of Sigmund Freud* (Vol. 23, pp. 209–254). London, England: Hogarth. (Original work published 1937)

Friedlander, M. L. (2015). Use of relational strategies to repair alliance ruptures: How responsive supervisors train responsive psychotherapists. *Psychotherapy: Theory, Research, & Practice, 52*, 174–179.

Friedlander, M. L., Escudero, V., Heatherington, L., & Diamond, G. M. (2011). Alliance in couple and family therapy. In J. C. Norcross (Ed.), *Psychotherapy relationships that work* (2nd ed., pp. 92–109). New York, NY: Oxford University Press. http://dx.doi.org/10.1093/acprof:oso/9780199737208.003.0004

Garfield, S. L. (1992). Eclectic psychotherapy: A common factors approach. In J. C. Norcross & M. R. Goldfried (Eds.), *Handbook of psychotherapy integration* (pp. 168–201). New York, NY: Basic Books.

Garfield, S. L., & Kurtz, R. (1977). A study of eclectic views. *Journal of Consulting and Clinical Psychology, 45*, 78–83. http://dx.doi.org/10.1037/0022-006X.45.1.78

Geller, J. D., Norcross, J. C., & Orlinsky, D. E. (Eds.). (2005). *The psychotherapist's own psychotherapy: Patient and clinician perspectives*. New York, NY: Oxford University Press.

Goldberg, D. A. (1985). Process notes, audio, and videotape: Modes of presentation in psychotherapy training. *The Clinical Supervisor, 3*(3), 3–14. http://dx.doi.org/10.1300/J001v03n03_02

Goldfried, M. R. (1980). Toward the delineation of therapeutic change principles. *American Psychologist, 35*, 991–999. http://dx.doi.org/10.1037/0003-066X.35.11.991

Goldfried, M. R. (Ed.). (2001). *How therapists change: Personal and professional reflections*. Washington, DC: American Psychological Association. http://dx.doi.org/10.1037/10392-000

Goldfried, M. R., Pachankis, J. E., & Bell, A. C. (2005). History of psychotherapy integration. In J. C. Norcross & M. R. Goldfried (Eds.), *Handbook of psychotherapy integration* (2nd ed., pp. 24–60). New York, NY: Oxford University Press. http://dx.doi.org/10.1093/med:psych/9780195165791.003.0002

Goldner-deBeer, L. (1999). *Psychotherapy integration in doctoral training programs: Are students prepared for the future?* (Unpublished doctoral dissertation). University of Denver, Denver, CO.

Grant, J., & Schofield, M. (2007). Career-long supervision: Patterns and perspectives. *Counseling and Psychotherapy Research, 7*, 3–11.

Gray, L. A., Ladany, N., Walker, J. A., & Ancis, J. R. (2001). Psychotherapy trainees' experience of counterproductive events in supervision. *Journal of Counseling Psychology, 48*, 371–383. http://dx.doi.org/10.1037/0022-0167.48.4.371

Grencavage, L. M., & Norcross, J. C. (1990). Where are the commonalities among the therapeutic common factors? *Professional Psychology: Research and Practice, 21*, 372–378. http://dx.doi.org/10.1037/0735-7028.21.5.372

Grey, A., & Fiscalini, J. (1987). Parallel process as transference-countertransference interaction. *Psychoanalytic Psychology*, 4, 131–144. http://dx.doi.org/10.1037/h0079131

Guest, P. D., & Beutler, L. E. (1988). The impact of psychotherapy supervision on therapist orientation and values. *Journal of Consulting and Clinical Psychology*, 56, 653–658. http://dx.doi.org/10.1037/0022-006X.56.5.653

Halford, G. S., Baker, R., McCredden, J. E., & Bain, J. D. (2005). How many variables can humans process? *Psychological Science*, 16, 70–76. http://dx.doi.org/10.1111/j.0956-7976.2005.00782.x

Halgin, R. P. (1985). Pragmatic blending of clinical models in the supervisory relationship. *The Clinical Supervisor*, 3, 23–46. http://dx.doi.org/10.1300/J001v03n04_03

Halgin, R. P. (Chair). (1986, May). *Issues in the supervision of integrative psychotherapy*. A symposium presented at the second annual meeting of the Society for the Exploration of Psychotherapy Integration, Toronto, Ontario, Canada.

Halgin, R. P. (Ed.). (1988). Issues in the supervision of integrative psychotherapy [Special section]. *Journal of Integrative & Eclectic Psychotherapy*, 7, 152–180.

Halgin, R. P., & McEntee, D. J. (1993). Countertransference dilemmas in integrative psychotherapy. In G. Stricker & J. Gold (Eds.), *Comprehensive textbook of psychotherapy integration* (pp. 513–522). New York, NY: Plenum Press.

Halgin, R. P., & Murphy, R. A. (1995). Issues in the training of psychotherapists. In B. M. Bongar & L. E. Beutler (Eds.), *Oxford textbooks in clinical psychology: Vol. 1. Comprehensive textbook of psychotherapy: Theory and practice* (pp. 434–455). New York, NY: Oxford University Press.

Handley, P. (1982). Relationship between supervisors' and trainees' cognitive styles and the supervision process. *Journal of Counseling Psychology*, 29, 508–515. http://dx.doi.org/10.1037/0022-0167.29.5.508

Hayes, J. A., Gelso, C. J., & Hummel, A. M. (2011). Managing countertransference. In J. C. Norcross (Ed.), *Psychotherapy relationships that work* (2nd ed., pp. 239–258). New York, NY: Oxford University Press. http://dx.doi.org/10.1093/acprof:oso/9780199737208.003.0012

Heide, F. J., & Rosenbaum, R. (1988). Therapist's experiences of using single versus combined theoretical models in psychotherapy. *Journal of Integrative & Eclectic Psychotherapy*, 7, 41–46.

Henry, W. E., Sims, J. H., & Spray, S. L. (1971). *The fifth profession: Becoming a psychotherapist*. San Francisco, CA: Jossey-Bass.

Heppner, P. P., & Roehlke, J. J. (1984). Differences among supervisees at different levels of training: Implications for a developmental model of supervision. *Journal of Counseling Psychology*, 31, 76–90. http://dx.doi.org/10.1037/0022-0167.31.1.76

# REFERENCES

Hess, A. K. (Ed.). (1980). *Psychotherapy supervision.* New York, NY: Wiley.

Hilsenroth, M. (Ed.). (2015). Progress monitoring and feedback [Special issue]. *Psychotherapy, 52,* 381–462.

Hilsenroth, M. J., Defife, J. A., Blagys, M. D., & Ackerman, S. J. (2006). Effects of training in short-term psychodynamic psychotherapy: Change in graduate clinician technique. *Psychotherapy Research, 16,* 293–305.

Hogan, R. A. (1964). Issues and approaches in supervision. *Psychotherapy: Theory, Research & Practice, 1,* 139–141. http://dx.doi.org/10.1037/h0088589

Holloway, E. L., & Wampold, B. E. (1986). Relation between conceptual level and counseling-related tasks: A meta-analysis. *Journal of Counseling Psychology, 33,* 310–319. http://dx.doi.org/10.1037/0022-0167.33.3.310

Holt, H., Beutler, L. E., Kimpara, S., Macias, S., Haug, N. A., Shiloff, N., . . . Stein, M. (2015). Evidence-based supervision: Tracking outcome and teaching principles of change in clinical supervision to bring science to integrative practice. *Psychotherapy, 52,* 185–189. http://dx.doi.org/10.1037/a0038732

Horvath, A. O., Del Re, A. C., Flückiger, C., & Symonds, D. (2011). Alliance in individual psychotherapy. In J. C. Norcross (Ed.), *Psychotherapy relationships that work* (2nd ed., pp. 25–69). New York, NY: Oxford University Press. http://dx.doi.org/10.1093/acprof:oso/9780199737208.003.0002

Horvath, A. O., & Greenberg, L. S. (1989). Development and validation of the Working Alliance Inventory. *Journal of Counseling Psychology, 36,* 223–233. http://dx.doi.org/10.1037/0022-0167.36.2.223

Hunsley, J., & Marsh, H. (2008). *A guide to assessments that work.* New York, NY: Oxford University Press.

Inman, A. G., & DeBoer Kreider, E. (2013). Multicultural competence: Psychotherapy practice and supervision. *Psychotherapy, 50,* 346–350. http://dx.doi.org/10.1037/a0032029

Inman, A. G., & Ladany, N. (2014). Multicultural competencies in psychotherapy supervision. In F. T. L. Leong (Ed.), *APA handbook of multicultural psychology: Vol. 2. Applications and training* (pp. 643–658). Washington, DC: American Psychological Association.

Jacobs, S. C., Huprich, S. K., Grus, C. L., Cage, E. A., Elman, N. S., Forrest, L., . . . Kaslow, N. J. (2011). Trainees with professional competency problems: Preparing trainers for difficult but necessary conversations. *Training and Education in Professional Psychology, 5,* 175–184. http://dx.doi.org/10.1037/a0024656

Kagan, N. (1980). Influencing human interaction: Eighteen years with IPR. In A. K. Hess (Ed.), *Psychotherapy supervision* (pp. 262–283). New York, NY: Wiley.

Kaslow, N. J. (2004). Competencies in professional psychology. *American Psychologist, 59,* 774–781. http://dx.doi.org/10.1037/0003-066X.59.8.774

Kaslow, N. J., Falender, C. A., & Grus, C. L. (2012). Valuing and practicing competency-based supervision: A transformational leadership perspective. *Training and Education in Professional Psychology, 6,* 47–54. http://dx.doi.org/10.1037/a0026704

Knox, S., Burkard, A. W., Edwards, L. M., Smith, J. J., & Schlosser, L. Z. (2008). Supervisors' reports of the effects of supervisor self-disclosure on supervisees. *Psychotherapy Research, 18,* 543–559.

Koocher, G. P., McMann, M. R., Stout, A. O., & Norcross, J. C. (2015). Discredited assessment and treatment methods used with children and adolescents: A Delphi Poll. *Journal of Clinical Child and Adolescent Psychology, 44,* 722–729.

Kopp, S. (1985). *Even a stone can be a teacher: Learning and growing from the experiences of everyday life.* Los Angeles, CA: Jeremy P. Tarcher.

Kuhn, T. S. (1970). *The structure of scientific revolutions* (2nd ed.). Chicago, IL: University of Chicago.

Ladany, N., Constantine, M. G., Miller, K., Erickson, C. D., & Muse-Burke, J. L. (2000). Supervisor countertransference: A qualitative investigation into its identification and description. *Journal of Counseling Psychology, 47,* 102–115. http://dx.doi.org/10.1037/0022-0167.47.1.102

Ladany, N., Friedlander, M. L., & Nelson, M. L. (2005). Remediating skill difficulties and deficits: It's more than just teaching. In N. Ladany, M. L. Friedlander, & M. L. Nelson (Eds.), *Critical events in supervision: An interpersonal approach* (pp. 23–51). Washington, DC: American Psychological Association. http://dx.doi.org/10.1037/10958-002

Ladany, N., Hill, C. E., Corbett, M. M., & Nutt, E. A. (1996). Nature, extent, and importance of what psychotherapy trainees do not disclose to their supervisors. *Journal of Counseling Psychology, 43,* 10–24. http://dx.doi.org/10.1037/0022-0167.43.1.10

Lambert, M. J. (2010). *Prevention of treatment failure: The use of measuring, monitoring, and feedback in clinical practice.* Washington, DC: American Psychological Association.

Lambert, M. J., & Ogles, B. M. (1997). The effectiveness of psychotherapy supervision. In C. E. Watkins, Jr. (Ed.), *Handbook of psychotherapy supervision* (pp. 421–446). New York, NY: Wiley.

Lambert, M. J., & Shimokawa, K. (2011). Collecting client feedback. In J. C. Norcross (Ed.), *Psychotherapy relationships that work* (2nd ed., pp. 203–223). New York, NY: Oxford University Press. http://dx.doi.org/10.1093/acprof:oso/9780199737208.003.0010

Lampropoulos, G. K. (2003). A common factors view of counseling supervision process. *The Clinical Supervisor, 21,* 77–95. http://dx.doi.org/10.1300/J001v21n01_06

Lampropoulos, G. K., & Dixon, D. N. (2007). Psychotherapy integration in internships and counseling psychology doctoral programs. *Journal of Psychotherapy Integration, 17*, 185–208. http://dx.doi.org/10.1037/1053-0479.17.2.185

Lazarus, A. A. (1967). In support of technical eclecticism. *Psychological Reports, 21*, 415–416. http://dx.doi.org/10.2466/pr0.1967.21.2.415

Lazarus, A. A. (1971). Where do behavior therapists take their troubles? *Psychological Reports, 28*, 349–350. http://dx.doi.org/10.2466/pr0.1971.28.2.349

Lazarus, A. A., Beutler, L. E., & Norcross, J. C. (1992). The future of technical eclecticism. *Psychotherapy: Theory, Research, Practice, Training, 29*, 11–20. http://dx.doi.org/10.1037/0033-3204.29.1.11

Levenson, H. (2012). Time-limited dynamic psychotherapy: An integrative perspective. In M. J. Dewan, B. N. Steenbarger, & R. P. Greenberg, *The art and science of brief psychotherapies: An illustrated guide* (2nd ed., pp. 195–238). Washington, DC: American Psychiatric Press.

Lichtenberg, J. W., Goodyear, R. K., Overland, E., Hutman, H., & Norcross, J. C. (2016). *Portrait of a specialty: Counseling psychology in the U.S. in relation to clinical psychology and to itself across three decades.* Manuscript submitted for publication.

Liff, Z. A. (1992). Psychoanalysis and dynamic techniques. In D. K. Freedheim (Ed.), *History of psychotherapy* (pp. 571–586). Washington, DC: American Psychological Association.

Lilienfeld, S. O. (2007). Psychological treatments that cause harm. *Perspectives on Psychological Science, 2*, 53–70. http://dx.doi.org/10.1111/j.1745-6916.2007.00029.x

Loganbill, C., Hardy, E., & Delworth, U. (1982). Supervision: A conceptual model. *The Counseling Psychologist, 10*(1), 3–42. http://dx.doi.org/10.1177/0011000082101002

London, P. (1966). Major issues in psychotherapy integration. *International Journal of Eclectic Psychotherapy, 5*(3), 1–12.

Lunde, D. T. (1974). Eclectic and integrated theory: Gordon Allport and others. In A. Burton (Ed.), *Operational theories of personality* (pp. 381–404). New York, NY: Brunner/Mazel.

Magnavita, J. J., & Anchin, J. C. (2014). *Unifying psychotherapy: Principles, methods, and evidence from clinical science.* New York, NY: Springer.

Maguire, G. P., Goldberg, D. P., Hobson, R. F., Margison, F., Moss, S., & O'Dowd, T. (1984). Evaluating the teaching of a method of psychotherapy. *The British Journal of Psychiatry, 144*, 575–580. http://dx.doi.org/10.1192/bjp.144.6.575

Mahoney, M. J. (1986). The tyranny of technique. *Counseling and Values, 30*, 169–174. http://dx.doi.org/10.1002/j.2161-007X.1986.tb00461.x

McNeill, B. W., & Stoltenberg, C. D. (2016). *Supervision essentials for the integrative developmental model.* Washington, DC: American Psychological Association. http://dx.doi.org/10.1037/14858-000

Mehr, K. E., Ladany, N., & Caskie, G. I. L. (2010). Trainee nondisclosure in supervision: What are they not telling you? *Counselling & Psychotherapy Research, 10,* 103–113. http://dx.doi.org/10.1080/14733141003712301

Meltzoff, J. (1984). Research training for clinical psychologists: Point—counterpoint. *Professional Psychology: Research and Practice, 15,* 203–209. http://dx.doi.org/10.1037/0735-7028.15.2.203

Messer, S. B. (1992). A critical examination of belief structures in integrative and eclectic psychotherapy. In J. C. Norcross & M. R. Goldfried (Eds.), *Handbook of psychotherapy integration* (pp. 130–168). New York, NY: Basic Books.

Messer, S. B. (2001). Introduction to the special issue on assimilative integration. *Journal of Psychotherapy Integration, 11,* 1–4. http://dx.doi.org/10.1023/A:1026619423048

Milne, D., Aylott, H., Fitzpatrick, H., & Ellis, M. V. (2008). How does clinical supervision work? Using a "best evidence synthesis" approach to construct a basic model of supervision. *The Clinical Supervisor, 27,* 170–190. http://dx.doi.org/10.1080/07325220802487915

Moskowitz, S. A., & Rupert, P. A. (1983). Conflict resolution within the supervisory relationship. *Professional Psychology: Research and Practice, 14,* 632–641. http://dx.doi.org/10.1037/0735-7028.14.5.632

Murphy, G. (1969). Psychology in the year 2000. *American Psychologist, 24,* 523–530. http://dx.doi.org/10.1037/h0027871

Nathan, P. E., & Gorman, J. M. (Eds.). (2015). *A guide to treatments that work* (4th ed.). New York, NY: Oxford University Press.

Nelson, G. (1978). Psychotherapy supervision from the trainee's point of view: A survey of preferences. *Professional Psychology, 9,* 539–550. http://dx.doi.org/10.1037/0735-7028.9.4.539

Nelson, M. L., Barnes, K. L., Evans, A. L., & Triggiano, P. J. (2008). Working with conflict in clinical supervision: Wise supervisors' perspectives. *Journal of Counseling Psychology, 55,* 172–184. http://dx.doi.org/10.1037/0022-0167.55.2.172

Nelson, M. L., & Friedlander, M. L. (2001). A close look at conflictual supervisory relationships: The trainee's perspective. *Journal of Counseling Psychology, 48,* 384–395.

Nettles, R., & Balter, R. (2011). *Multiple minority identities.* New York, NY: Springer.

Neufeldt, S. A., Beutler, L. E., & Banchero, R. (1997). Research on supervisor variables in psychotherapy research. In C. E. Watkins, Jr. (Ed.), *Handbook of psychotherapy supervision* (pp. 508–524). New York, NY: Wiley.

# REFERENCES

Norcross, J. C. (Ed.). (1986). Training integrative/eclectic psychotherapists [Special section]. *International Journal of Eclectic Psychotherapy, 5*, 71–94.

Norcross, J. C. (1988). Supervision of integrative psychotherapy. *Journal of Integrative & Eclectic Psychotherapy, 7*, 157–166.

Norcross, J. C. (1990, August). *Countertransference confessions of a prescriptive eclectic.* Paper presented at the annual conference of the Society for the Exploration of Psychotherapy Integration, Philadelphia, PA.

Norcross, J. C. (2000). Psychotherapist self-care: Practitioner-tested, research-informed strategies. *Professional Psychology: Research and Practice, 31*, 710–713. http://dx.doi.org/10.1037/0735-7028.31.6.710

Norcross, J. C. (2005). The psychotherapist's own psychotherapy: Educating and developing psychologists. *American Psychologist, 60*, 840–850. http://dx.doi.org/10.1037/0003-066X.60.8.840

Norcross, J. C. (2006). Personal integration: An N of 1 study. *Journal of Psychotherapy Integration, 16*, 59–72. http://dx.doi.org/10.1037/1053-0479.16.1.59

Norcross, J. C. (Ed.). (2011). *Psychotherapy relationships that work* (2nd ed.). New York, NY: Oxford University Press. http://dx.doi.org/10.1093/acprof:oso/9780199737208.001.0001

Norcross, J. C., & Aboyoun, D. C. (1994). Self-change experiences of psychotherapists. In T. M. Brinthaupt & R. P. Lipka (Eds.), *Changing the self* (pp. 253–278). Albany: State University of New York Press.

Norcross, J. C., & Beutler, L. E. (2000). A prescriptive eclectic approach to psychotherapy training. *Journal of Psychotherapy Integration, 10*, 247–261. http://dx.doi.org/10.1023/A:1009444912173

Norcross, J. C., & Beutler, L. E. (2014). Evidence-based relationships and responsiveness for depression and substance abuse. In D. H. Barlow (Ed.), *Clinical handbook of psychological disorders* (5th ed., pp. 617–639). New York, NY: Guilford.

Norcross, J. C., Beutler, L. E., & Clarkin, J. F. (1990). Training in differential treatment selection. In L. E. Beutler & J. F. Clarkin (Eds.), *Systematic treatment selection: Toward targeted therapeutic intervention* (pp. 289–307). New York, NY: Brunner/Mazel.

Norcross, J. C., Beutler, L. E., Clarkin, J. F., DiClemente, C. C., Halgin, R. P., Frances, A., . . . Suedfeld, P. (1986). Training integrative/eclectic psychotherapists. *Journal of Integrative & Eclectic Psychotherapy, 5*, 71–94.

Norcross, J. C., Beutler, L. E., & Levant, R. F. (Eds.). (2006). *Evidence-based practices in mental health: Debate and dialogue on the fundamental questions.* Washington, DC: American Psychological Association. http://dx.doi.org/10.1037/11265-000

Norcross, J. C., Campbell, L. M., Grohol, J. M., Santrock, J. W., Selagea, F., & Sommer, R. (2013). *Self-help that works: Resources to improve emotional health and strengthen relationships* (4th ed.). New York, NY: Oxford University Press.

Norcross, J. C., Dryden, W., & DeMichele, J. T. (1992). British clinical psychologists and personal therapy: III. What's good for the goose? *Clinical Psychology Forum, 44*, 29–33.

Norcross, J. C., & Goldfried, M. R. (Eds.). (2005). *Handbook of psychotherapy integration* (2nd ed.). New York, NY: Oxford University Press. http://dx.doi.org/10.1093/med:psych/9780195165791.001.0001

Norcross, J. C., & Guy, J. D. (2005). The prevalence and parameters of personal therapy in the US. In J. D. Geller, J. C. Norcross, & D. E. Orlinksy (Eds.), *The psychotherapist's own psychotherapy: Patient and clinician perspectives* (pp. 165–176). New York, NY: Oxford University Press.

Norcross, J. C., & Guy, J. D. (Eds.). (2007). *Leaving it at the office: A guide to psychotherapist self-care.* New York, NY: Guilford.

Norcross, J. C., & Halgin, R. P. (1997). Integrative approaches to psychotherapy supervision. In C. E. Watkins, Jr. (Ed.), *Handbook of psychotherapy supervision* (pp. 203–222). New York, NY: Wiley.

Norcross, J. C., Hogan, T. P., Koocher, G. P., & Maggio, L. (2017). *Clinician's guide to evidence-based practice: Behavioral health and addictions* (2nd ed.). New York, NY: Oxford University Press.

Norcross, J. C., Karpiak, C. P., & Lister, K. M. (2005). What's an integrationist? A study of self-identified integrative and (occasionally) eclectic psychologists. *Journal of Clinical Psychology, 61*, 1587–1594. http://dx.doi.org/10.1002/jclp.20203

Norcross, J. C., Koocher, G. P., & Garofalo, A. (2006). Discredited psychological treatments and tests: A Delphi poll. *Professional Psychology, Research and Practice, 37*, 515–522. http://dx.doi.org/10.1037/0735-7028.37.5.515

Norcross, J. C., Krebs, P. M., & Prochaska, J. O. (2011). Stages of change. In J. C. Norcross (Ed.), *Psychotherapy relationships that work* (2nd ed., pp. 279–300). New York, NY: Oxford University Press. http://dx.doi.org/10.1093/acprof:oso/9780199737208.003.0014

Norcross, J. C., & Lambert, M. J. (2014). Relationship science and practice in psychotherapy: Closing commentary. *Psychotherapy, 51*, 398–403. http://dx.doi.org/10.1037/a0037418

Norcross, J. C., Pfund, R. A., & Prochaska, J. O. (2013). Psychotherapy in 2022: A Delphi poll on its future. *Professional Psychology: Research and Practice, 44*, 363–370. http://dx.doi.org/10.1037/a0034633

Norcross, J. C., & Prochaska, J. O. (1988). A study of eclectic (and integrative) views revisited. *Professional Psychology: Research and Practice, 19*, 170–174. http://dx.doi.org/10.1037/0735-7028.19.2.170

Norcross, J. C., & Rogan, J. D. (2013). Psychologists conducting psychotherapy in 2012: Current practices and historical trends among Division 29 members. *Psychotherapy, 50*, 490–495. http://dx.doi.org/10.1037/a0033512

Norcross, J. C., & Sayette, M. A. (2016). *Insider's guide to graduate programs in clinical and counseling psychology (2016/2017 edition)*. New York, NY: Guilford Press.

Norcross, J. C., & VandenBos, G. R. (2011). Training audiotapes and videotapes. In J. C. Norcross, G. R. VandenBos, & D. K. Freedheim (Eds.), *History of psychotherapy* (2nd ed., pp. 693–702). Washington, DC: American Psychological Association. http://dx.doi.org/10.1037/12353-046

Norcross, J. C., Zimmerman, B. E., Greenberg, R., & Swift, J. K. (2016). *Do all therapists do that when saying goodbye? A study of commonalities in termination behaviors*. Manuscript submitted for publication.

Omer, H., & London, P. (1988). Metamorphosis in psychotherapy: End of the systems era. *Psychotherapy: Theory, Research, Practice, Training, 25*, 171–180. http://dx.doi.org/10.1037/h0085329

Orlinsky, D. E., & Norcross, J. C. (2005). Outcomes and impacts of the psychotherapists' personal therapy: A research review. In J. D. Geller, J. C. Norcross, & D. E. Orlinsky (Eds.), *The psychotherapist's own psychotherapy: Patient and clinician perspectives* (pp. 214–230). New York, NY: Oxford University Press.

Orlinsky, D. E., & Rønnestad, M. H. (2005). *How psychotherapists develop: A study of therapeutic work and professional growth*. Washington, DC: American Psychological Association. http://dx.doi.org/10.1037/11157-000

Osler, W. (1906). *Aequanimatas*. New York, NY: McGraw-Hill.

Page, S., & Wosket, V. (Eds.). (2001). *Supervising the counsellor: A cyclical model* (2nd ed.). Hove, England: Brunner-Routledge.

Paniagua, F. A. (2005). *Assessing and treating culturally diverse clients: A practical guide* (3rd ed.). Thousand Oaks, CA: Sage. http://dx.doi.org/10.4135/9781483329093

Peake, T. H., Nussbaum, B. D., & Tindell, S. D. (2002). Clinical and counseling supervision references: Trends and needs. *Psychotherapy: Theory, Research, Practice, Training, 39*, 114–125. http://dx.doi.org/10.1037/0033-3204.39.1.114

Persons, J. B., Hong, J. J., Eidelman, P., & Owen, D. J. (2016). Learning from practice and patients. In J. C. Norcross, G. R. VandenBos, & D. K. Freedheim (Eds.), *APA handbook of clinical psychology: Vol. 5. Education and profession* (pp. 255–268). Washington, DC: American Psychological Association.

Phillips, G. L., & Kanter, C. N. (1984). Mutuality in psychotherapy supervision. *Psychotherapy: Theory, Research, Practice, Training, 21*, 178–183. http://dx.doi.org/10.1037/h0085969

Pope, K. S., & Vasquez, M. J. T. (2016). *Ethics in psychotherapy and counseling: A practical guide* (5th ed.). Hoboken, NJ: Wiley.

Prochaska, J. O. (1979). *Systems of psychotherapy: A transtheoretical analysis*. Homewood, IL: Dorsey.

Prochaska, J. O., & DiClemente, C. C. (1984). *The transtheoretical approach: Crossing the traditional boundaries of therapy.* Homewood, IL: Dow Jones-Irvin.

Prochaska, J. O., & Norcross, J. C. (1983). Psychotherapists' perspectives on treating themselves and their clients for psychic distress. *Professional Psychology, 14,* 642–655.

Prochaska, J. O., & Norcross, J. C. (2013). *Systems of psychotherapy: A transtheoretical analysis* (8th ed.). Pacific Grove, CA: Cengage-Brooks/Cole.

Ramos-Sánchez, L., Esnil, E., Goodwin, A., Riggs, S., Touster, L. O., Wright, L. K., . . . Rodolfa, E. (2002). Negative supervisory events: Effects on supervision and supervisory alliance. *Professional Psychology: Research and Practice, 33,* 197–202. http://dx.doi.org/10.1037/0735-7028.33.2.197

Reichelt, S., & Skjerve, J. (2002). Correspondence between supervisors and trainees in their perception of supervision events. *Journal of Clinical Psychology, 58,* 759–772. http://dx.doi.org/10.1002/jclp.2003

Robertson, M. (1979). Some observations from an eclectic therapist. *Psychotherapy: Theory, Research & Practice, 16,* 18–21. http://dx.doi.org/10.1037/h0085867

Robiner, W. N., Fuhrman, M., & Ristvedt, S. (1993). Evaluation and difficulties in supervising psychology interns. *The Clinical Psychologist, 46,* 3–13.

Rosen, C. S. (2000). Is the sequencing of change processes by stage consistent across health problems? A meta-analysis. *Health Psychology, 19,* 593–604. http://dx.doi.org/10.1037/0278-6133.19.6.593

Rosenbaum, R. (1988). Feelings toward integration: A matter of style and identity. *Journal of Integrative & Eclectic Psychotherapy, 7,* 52–60.

Rosenblatt, A., & Mayer, J. E. (1975). Objectionable supervisory styles: Students' views. *Social Work, 20,* 184–189.

Rosenzweig, S. (1936). Some implicit common factors in diverse methods in psychotherapy. *American Journal of Orthopsychiatry, 6,* 412–415.

Ryle, A. (1990). *Cognitive-analytic therapy: Active participation in change.* Chichester, England: Wiley.

Sacuzzo, D. (2003). *Liability for failure to supervise adequately: Let the master beware.* The National Register of Health Service Providers in Psychology, Legal Update 13.

Safran, J. D., & Muran, J. C. (2000). *Negotiating the therapeutic alliance: A relational treatment guide.* New York, NY: Guilford Press.

Safran, J. D., Muran, J. C., & Eubanks-Carter, C. (2011). Repairing alliance ruptures. In J. C. Norcross (Ed.), *Psychotherapy relationships that work* (2nd ed., pp. 224–238). New York, NY: Oxford University Press. http://dx.doi.org/10.1093/acprof:oso/9780199737208.003.0011

# REFERENCES

Saltzman, N., & Norcross, J. C. (Eds.). (1990). *Therapy wars: Contention and convergence in differing clinical approaches.* San Francisco, CA: Jossey-Bass.

Sarnat, J. E. (1992). Supervision in relationship: Resolving the teach–treat controversy in psychoanalytic supervision. *Psychoanalytic Psychology, 9,* 387–403.

Sarnat, J. E. (2015). *Supervision essentials for psychodynamic psychotherapies.* Washington, DC: American Psychological Association.

Schacht, T. E. (1991). Can psychotherapy education advance psychotherapy integration? A view from the cognitive psychology of expertise. *Journal of Psychotherapy Integration, 1,* 305–319. http://dx.doi.org/10.1037/h0101194

Schottenbauer, M. A., Glass, C. R., & Arnkoff, D. B. (2005). Outcome research on psychotherapy integration. In J. C. Norcross & M. R. Goldfried (Eds.), *Handbook of psychotherapy integration* (2nd ed., pp. 459–493). New York, NY: Oxford University Press. http://dx.doi.org/10.1093/med:psych/9780195165791.003.0022

Schultz-Ross, R. A. (1995). Ideological singularity as a defense against clinical complexity. *American Journal of Psychotherapy, 49,* 540–547.

Shanfield, S. B., Hetherly, V. V., & Matthews, K. L. (2001). Excellent supervision: The residents' perspective. *Journal of Psychotherapy Practice and Research, 10,* 23–27.

Shapiro, S. J. (1986). Thought experiments for psychotherapists. *International Journal of Eclectic Psychotherapy, 5*(1), 69–70.

Shirk, S. R., & Karver, M. (2011). Alliance in child and adolescent therapy. In J. C. Norcross (Ed.), *Psychotherapy relationships that work* (2nd ed., pp. 70–91). New York, NY: Oxford University Press. http://dx.doi.org/10.1093/acprof:oso/9780199737208.003.0003

Smith, T. B., Rodriguez, M. D., & Bernal, G. (2011). Culture. In J. C. Norcross (Ed.), *Psychotherapy relationships that work* (2nd ed., pp. 316–335). New York, NY: Oxford University Press. http://dx.doi.org/10.1093/acprof:oso/9780199737208.003.0016

Stanovich, K. E., West, R. W., & Toplak, M. E. (2013). Myside bias, rational thinking, and intelligence. *Current Directions in Psychological Science, 22,* 259–264. http://dx.doi.org/10.1177/0963721413480174

Stein, M., Beutler, L. E., Kimpara, S., Haug, N., Brunet, H., Someah, K., Edwards, C. J., & Macias, S. (2016). *The impact of a common factors, principle-based supervisory approach on treatment outcomes at a psychology training clinic.* Manuscript submitted for publication.

Stoltenberg, C. D., & Delworth, U. (1987). *Supervising counselors and therapists: A developmental approach.* San Francisco, CA: Jossey-Bass.

Stricker, G. (1988). Supervision of integrative psychotherapy. *Journal of Integrative & Eclectic Psychotherapy, 7,* 176–180.

# REFERENCES

Stricker, G., & Gold, J. (1996). An assimilative model of psychodynamically oriented integrative psychotherapy. *Clinical Psychology: Science and Practice, 3,* 47–58.

Sulloway, F. J. (1996). *Born to rebel: Birth order, family dynamics, and creative lives.* New York, NY: Pantheon.

Swift, J. K., Callahan, J. L., & Vollmer, B. M. (2011). Preferences. In J. C. Norcross (Ed.), *Psychotherapy relationships that work* (2nd ed., pp. 301–315). New York, NY: Oxford University Press. http://dx.doi.org/10.1093/acprof:oso/9780199737208.003.0015

Tennen, H. (1988). Supervision of integrative psychotherapy: A critique. *Journal of Integrative & Eclectic Psychotherapy, 7,* 167–175.

Thorne, F. C. (1957). Critique of recent developments in personality counseling theory. *Journal of Clinical Psychology, 13,* 234–244. http://dx.doi.org/10.1002/1097-4679(195707)13:3<234::AID-JCLP2270130304>3.0.CO;2-O

Thorne, F. C. (1967). The structure of integrative psychology. *Journal of Clinical Psychology, 23,* 3–11. http://dx.doi.org/10.1002/1097-4679(196701)23:1<3::AID-JCLP2270230102>3.0.CO;2-I

Tracey, T. J., Ellickson, J. L., & Sherry, P. (1989). Reactance in relation to different supervisory environments and counselor development. *Journal of Counseling Psychology, 36,* 336–344. http://dx.doi.org/10.1037/0022-0167.36.3.336

Tryon, G. S. (1996). Supervisee development during the practicum year. *Counselor Education and Supervision, 35,* 287–294. http://dx.doi.org/10.1002/j.1556-6978.1996.tb01929.x

Tryon, G. S., & Winograd, G. (2011). Goal consensus and collaboration. In J. C. Norcross (Ed.), *Psychotherapy relationships that work* (2nd ed., pp. 153–167). New York, NY: Oxford University Press. http://dx.doi.org/10.1093/acprof:oso/9780199737208.003.0007

Vaillant, L. M. (1997). *Changing character.* New York, NY: Basic Books.

Wachtel, P. L. (1977). *Psychoanalysis and behavior therapy: Toward an integration.* New York, NY: Basic Books.

Wachtel, P. L. (1987). *Action and insight.* New York, NY: Guilford Press.

Wachtel, P. L. (1991). From eclecticism to synthesis: Toward a more seamless psychotherapeutic integration. *Journal of Psychotherapy Integration, 1,* 43–54. http://dx.doi.org/10.1037/h0101201

Wainwright, N. A. (2010). *The development of the Leeds Alliance in Supervision Scale (LASS): A brief sessional measure of the supervisory alliance* (Unpublished doctoral dissertation). University of Leeds, England.

Wampold, B. E., & Imel, Z. E. (2015). *The great psychotherapy debate: The evidence for what makes psychotherapy work* (2nd ed.). New York, NY: Routledge.

Watkins, C. E., Jr. (1997). *Handbook of psychotherapy supervision.* New York, NY: Wiley.

Watkins, C. E., Jr. (2014). The supervisory alliance: A half century of theory, practice, and research in critical perspective. *American Journal of Psychotherapy*, 68, 19–55.

Watkins, C. E., Jr., Budge, S. L., & Callahan, J. L. (2015). Common and specific factors converging in psychotherapy supervision: A supervisory extrapolation of the Wampold/Budge psychotherapy relationship model. *Journal of Psychotherapy Integration*, 25, 214–235. http://dx.doi.org/10.1037/a0039561

Weinberger, J. (1995). Common factors aren't so common: The common factors dilemma. *Clinical Psychology: Science and Practice*, 2, 45–69. http://dx.doi.org/10.1111/j.1468-2850.1995.tb00024.x

Worthington, E. L. (1987). Changes in supervision as counselors and supervisors gain experience: A review. *Professional Psychology: Research and Practice*, 18, 189–208. http://dx.doi.org/10.1037/0735-7028.18.3.189

Youn, S. J., Castonguay, L. G., Xiao, H., Janis, R., McAleavey, A. A., Lockard, A. J., . . . Hayes, J. A. (2015). The Counseling Center Assessment of Psychological Symptoms (CCAPS): Merging clinical practice, training, and research. *Psychotherapy*, 52, 432–441. http://dx.doi.org/10.1037/pst0000029

Ziv-Beiman, S. (2014). Teaching psychotherapy integration from the start: A proposal to teach integration as a fundamental aspect. *Journal of Psychotherapy Integration*, 24, 251–257. http://dx.doi.org/10.1037/a0037800

# Index

Abuse of power, 109
Action-oriented therapies, 37
Adaptation(s)
   cultural, 110–111, 136–137
   to individual differences, 136–137
   supervisees' problems with, 105–106
   of supervisory methods, 65–66, 80–86, 134
   treatment, 90–96, 134
Advanced students, methods with, 81–82
Agendas, supervision sessions, 88
Alliance
   supervisory, 114–115
   therapeutic, 39–40
Ambiguity, 43
American Psychiatric Association, 13
American Psychological Association (APA)
   competency guidelines of, 18, 55
   definition of supervision by, 28
   guidance on supervision from, 4, 17
*Analysis Terminable and Interminable* (Freud), 122
Anxiety, of supervisees, 105
APA. *See* American Psychological Association

Assessment
   of supervisee needs, 66–67
   of transdiagnostic patient features, 34–35, 136
Assimilative integration, 11–12
Assimilative psychodynamic therapy, 11
Authoritarian relational style, 50, 104

Beginning interaction (supervision session), 88
Beginning students
   abuse of power with, 109
   adapting supervisory methods for, 81–82
Behavioral resistance, supervisees displaying, 104–105
Behaviors
   of supervisees and clients, 51–52
   of supervisors and therapists, 15–16
   therapeutic relationship-building, 40
Behavior therapists, personal therapy for, 122
Berg, Insoo Kim, 119
Beutler, Larry, 9
*Both/and* frame, 68, 75
Brief outpatient settings, 63

Case summaries, 70
Castonguay, Louis, 11
CCAPS (Counseling Center Assessment of Psychological Symptoms), 53
Challenges, supervisory, 103–115
    conflicts with supervisees, 113–115
    "difficult" supervisees, 103–107
    improving multicultural competence, 110–111
    legal and ethical matters, 111–113
    power struggles with supervisees, 109
    skill deficits, supervisees with, 107–108
Client(s)/Patient(s)
    behaviors of supervisees and, 51–52
    comfort of supervisees vs. needs of, 39
    evaluation of, 52–54
    feedback from, 53
    preferences of, 37–38, 90–96, 99–100
    therapists as, 124
    transdiagnostic features of. *See* Transdiagnostic patient features
    treatment fit for, 36–39, 113
    vulnerabilities, expressing, 98
Clinical setting
    adapting supervision to, 85–86
    for integrative supervision, 62–63
Clinical supervision
    goals of, 28
    outcome research on, 128–129
    in psychotherapy, 3–4
    supervisory relationship in, 15
Clinical Supervision Essentials series (APA), xiv, 4
Clinical urgencies, 88
Clinical work
    benefits of personal therapy for, 124
    supervisors', benefits of supervision for, 119

Cognitive–analytic therapy, 10
Cognitive–behavioral assimilative therapy, 11
Cognitive style, 83, 115
Cognitive therapy, 10
Collaborative supervision, 82
Comfort, supervisee, 39, 101
Common factors, 7–9
Competence
    as goal of supervision, 28–29
    in integrative psychotherapy, 30–31
    multicultural, improving, 110–111
    single-system, 29–30
    supervisees' consternation about, 43
    supervisor and supervisee, 4, 18
Competency(-ies)
    benchmarks in integrative supervision for, 135
    "difficult" supervisees with single-system, 104–105
    evaluation of supervisees', 54–55
Competency-based supervision, 17–18
Compliance, 36
Conceptual deficits, 107
Conceptual development, 83
Confidence, supervisee, 101
Conflict, with supervisees, 46, 113–115
Confusion stage, 82, 83
Consternation, supervisee, 41–44
Consultation, 74–75, 125
Context, for integrative supervision, 62–63
Contracts, 45–46, 114
Control, 109
Coping style, 37
Cosupervision, 74
Cotherapy, 69–70
Counseling Center Assessment of Psychological Symptoms (CCAPS), 53

# INDEX

Counterproductive supervisory events, 104
Countertransference, 43, 69
Critical incidents, reviews of, 70
Cultural identity, 84–85, 111
Culturally adapted supervision, 84–85
Culturally adapted treatments, 38, 136–137

Deep structure integration, 32
Defiance, 36
Developmental stage, supervisees', 81–83, 115
DiClemente, Carlo, 10, 14
"Difficult" supervisees, 103–107
Directiveness, 36, 84
Discredited treatments, offering, 112
Distance supervision, 135–136
Doctoral program students, 30
Documentation, 40, 79–80
Dropouts, 38, 99–100

EBP (evidence-based practice), 17, 34
Eclecticism, 9–11, 65–66
Eclectic supervision, 133–134
Ekstein, R., 120
Ellis, M. V., 128
Emotional reactions, modeling, 76–78
Emotional stress, 124
Ending interaction (supervision session), 100–101
Ethical issues, 111–113
Evaluation, 52–57
    of clients, 52–54
    conflict with supervisees about, 113–114
    of supervisees, 54–55
    of supervision, 57
    of supervisors, 55–57
Evidence-based practice (EBP), 17, 34
Evidence-based principles, for conducting supervision, 128–129
Expectations, 44–47

Expert therapists, integrative supervision with, 32
Externalizing coping style, 37

Falender, C. A., 46
Feedback
    from clients, 53
    in integrative supervision, xiv
    preventing conflict with, 114
    setting expectations about, 45–47
    from supervisees, 40–41, 57–62
    in systematic reflection, 72
Fit
    client–treatment, 36–39, 113
    in integrative psychotherapy, 7
    in integrative supervision, 27, 41
Flexibility, 5
Formative feedback, 54, 55
Frank, Jerome, 7
French, Thomas, 13
Freud, Sigmund, 12–13, 122
Friedlander, M. L., 79

*Getting the Most Out of Clinical Training and Supervision* (Falender & Shafranske), 46
Goals
    of integrative supervision, 28–33, 82
    of psychotherapy vs. supervision, 16
    and selection of supervisory methods, 68–69
Gold, Jerold, 11
Goldfried, Marvin, 8
Group therapy, 86

Heide, F. J., 41–42
Holmes, Oliver Wendell, Sr., 28

Identity, cultural, 84–85, 111
Incremental improvement, 61–62
Individual differences, adaptations to, 136–137
Individualization, in integrative psychotherapy, 4–5
Individual therapy, 86

# INDEX

InnerLife Systematic Treatment Selection, 53, 130, 136
Inpatient settings, 63
Instructing, 78–79
Integration stage, 82, 83
Integrative formulation, 90–96
Integrative psychotherapy
  assessment for, 35
  historical perspective on, 12–14
  integrative supervision for competence in, 30–31
  supervisee consternation with, 41–42
  supervision for trainees not adopting, 27–28
  supervision in single-school therapy systems vs., 4
  systematic models in, 67–68
  theory of, 5–7
  timing of exposure to, 31–32
*Integrative Psychotherapy Supervision* (DVD), xv, 4, 70
Integrative supervision, 27–63, 133–138
  of assessment of transdiagnostic patient features, 34–36
  challenges in, 103
  competency benchmarks for, 135
  context/setting for, 62–63
  creating rationale for, 66–68
  cultivating respect for research in, 33–34
  defined, xv
  distinctive features of, xiii, xiv
  evaluation in, 52–57
  feedback from supervisees in, 57–62
  functions of, 33–44
  future outcome research on, 137–138
  goals of, 28–33
  historical perspective on, 12–15
  individual and cultural differences in, 136–137
  methods specific to, 74–75
  outcome research on, 129–131
  promoting/tracking therapeutic relationship in, 39–41
  role of supervisory relationship in, 48–52
  setting expectations in, 44–47
  supervisees with behavioral resistance to, 104–105
  technology in, 135–136
  theoretical perspective on, 7–12
  of therapy implementation, 36–39
  timing for, 31–32
  understanding/managing supervisee consternation in, 41–44
Integrative treatment planning, 32–33
Internalizing coping style, 37
Interpersonal deficits, supervisees with, 107–108
Interpersonal style, 81

Kafka, Franz, 105

Laertius, Diogenes, 12
LASS (Leeds Alliance in Supervision Scale), 56
Lazarus, Arnold, 9, 13
Learning
  ongoing, by supervisors, 125
  from self-reflection, 72–73
  supervision in, 3
Leeds Alliance in Supervision Scale (LASS), 56
Legal issues, 111–113
Levenson, Hanna, 48, 70
Live observation, 70
London, P., 10
Loss, during termination sessions, 119

Mahoney, M. J., 48
Master's program enrollees, 30
Mental effort, of integrative psychotherapy/supervision, 42–44

# INDEX

Mental health professionals, personal therapy for, 123
Messer, Stanley, 11
Methods, supervisory, 65–86
 adaptation of, 65–66, 80–86
 and creating rationale for integrative supervision, 66–68
 in individual and group formats, 86
 instructing, 78–79
 modeling, 75–78
 providing documentation, 79–80
 research on effectiveness of, xiv
 selection of, 68–75
 tailoring of, xiv
Mistakes
 learning from, 72–73
 sharing, 47–49, 76, 118–119
Modeling
 of cultural sensitivity, 111
 in delivery of feedback, 61
 of interpersonal skills, 108
 method for, 75–78
 of self-care, 121
Monitoring
 of clients, 52–53
 of integrative supervision, xiv
 by supervisors and supervisees, 40–41
Multicultural competence, 110–111
Multimodal therapy, 9
Multiple hypotheses, constructing, 89–90
Multitheory comparison approach, 133
Murphy, Gardner, 4
Mutuality, 48, 82
Myside bias, 106

Needs, client, 39
Needs assessment, supervisee, 66–67
Nondisclosures, 98
Notes, process, 70
Novice therapists, integrative supervision with, 32

Observation(s)
 behind one-way mirrors, 70
 instruction and sharing of, 78–79
One-size-fits-all approach to psychotherapy, 4
One-way mirrors, 70
Ongoing learning (for supervisors), 125
Osler, William, 35
Outcome Questionnaire, 53
Outcome research, 127–131
 on client preferences, 37–38
 on clinical supervision, 128–129
 on coping style, 37
 cultivating respect for, 33–34
 on culture, 38
 on integrative supervision, 129–131
 on personal therapy for therapists, 123
 on psychotherapy, xiv
 on reactance level, 36
 on stages of change, 36–37
 on supervisory methods, xiv

Parallel process
 attending to, 96–98
 defined, 96
 for ending of sessions, 101
 in integrative supervision, 27, 52
 in psychotherapy and supervision, 51–52
Patients. *See* Client(s)
Peer-vision, 125
Pennsylvania
 professional development requirements in, 118
 supervisee evaluation requirements in, 55
Perfectionists, 106–107
Personal development activities, 124–125
Personal idiom, 85–86
Personality characteristics, adapting supervision to, 80

# INDEX

Personalization, of supervision sessions, 87
Personal problems, supervisees', 17
Personal therapy, 17, 122–124
Power struggles, 109
Pragmatic blending, 15
Preferences (client)
    adaptation to, 99–100
    implementing therapies based on, 37–38
    in supervision sessions, 90–96
Preferences (supervisee)
    adapting supervision to, 81
    consternation related to, 43
Process notes, 70
Prochaska, James, 10, 14
Professional development, 56, 118–120
*Psychoanalysis and Behavior Therapy* (Wachtel), 13–14
Psychoanalytic–behavioral therapy, 10
Psychotherapists. *See* Therapists
Psychotherapy. *See also* Integrative psychotherapy
    adapting supervision to, 83
    one-size-fits-all approach to, 4
    parallel processes between supervision and, 51–52
    supervising implementation of, 36–39
    supervision in, 3–4
    supervision vs., 15–17
    tailoring, to transdiagnostic patient features, 96
Psychotherapy Video Series (APA), 47

Reactance level, 36, 38, 84, 115
Readings, for supervisees, 46–47
Referrals, 17, 29–30
Reflection
    self-, 61–62, 72–73, 125
    systematic, 72–73
Relational instruction strategies, 79
Relational preferences
    of clients, 38
    of supervisors, 49–50
Relational style(s)
    fitting patient features with, 113
    supervisees with difficulty adapting, 105–106
    of supervisors, 49–50
Relationship
    supervisory. *See* Supervisory relationship
    therapeutic, 8, 39–41
Relationship factors, in supervisory relationship, 51
Remediation plans, 108
Remote and uncommitted relational style, 50
Research. *See* Outcome research
Respect, 33–34, 109
Responsibility, 109
Reviews of critical incidents, 70
Robertson, M, 105
Rosenbaum, R., 41–42
Rosenzweig, Saul, 13
Rupture resolution, 114–115
Ryle, Anthony, 10

Self-care, 120–122
Self-disclosure, 49, 76, 98
Self-reflection, 61–62, 72–73, 125
Session Rating Scale (SRS), 53
Shafranske, E. P., 46
Single-school therapy systems
    consternation with integrative vs., 41–42
    culture in, 110
    supervisees indoctrinated in, 104–105
    supervision in integrative psychotherapy vs., 4
Single-system competence, 29–30
Single-theory approach, 133
Skill deficits, supervisees with, 107–108
Socialization, 124

# INDEX

SRS (Session Rating Scale), 53
Stages of change, 36–37
Stagnation stage, 82, 83
Stamina, 42
Stress, emotional, 124
Stricker, George, 11
STS. *See* Systematic Treatment Selection
Successes, learning from, 72–73
Summaries, of supervision sessions, 100–101
Summative evaluations, 53, 55
Supervisee(s)
    behaviors of clients and, 51–52
    comfort of, 39, 101
    competence of, 4, 18
    conflicts with, 46, 113–115
    consternation of, 41–44
    developmental stage of, 81–83, 115
    "difficult," 103–107
    discussions of personal problems with, 17
    evaluation of, 54–55
    expectations for, 44–47
    expression of vulnerabilities by, 98
    feedback for, 57–62
    feedback from, 40–41, 57–59
    needs assessment for, 66–67
    perspective of, xiv
    power struggles with, 109
    self-care for, 120–121
    with skill deficits, 107–108
Supervision. *See also* Clinical supervision; Integrative supervision
    adapting, to personality characteristics, 80
    APA definition of, 28
    co-, 74
    collaborative, 82
    competency-based, 17–18
    as core competency, 135
    culturally adapted, 84–85
    defined, 15–18
    distance, 135–136
    eclectic, 133–134
    evaluation of, 57
    evidence-based principles for conducting, 128–129
    parallel processes between psychotherapy and, 51–52
    psychotherapy vs., 15–17
    of supervision, 125
    theoretical integration and eclecticism in, 10–11
    of virtual therapies, 135–136
"Super-vision," 119
Supervision sessions, 87–100
    attending to parallel processes in, 96–98
    beginning interaction in, 88
    construction of multiple hypotheses in, 89–90
    ending interaction in, 100–101
    on integrative formulation and treatment adaptation, 90–96
    on termination of therapy, 99–100
Supervisors, 117–125
    behaviors of therapists and, 15–16
    competence of, 4, 18
    and "difficult" supervisees, 104
    evaluation of, 55–57
    ongoing learning and consultation by, 125
    personal development activities of, 124–125
    personal therapy for, 122–124
    professional development of, 118–120
    relational preferences of, 49–50
    responsibilities of, 108
    roles of, 33
    self-care for, 120–122
    training for, 117–118
    vulnerability of, 76, 118–119
Supervisory methods. *See* Methods, supervisory

# INDEX

Supervisory relationship
  in clinical supervision, 15
  effects of poor, 50–51
  expectations about, 45–46
  resolving conflicts and, 114–115
  role of, 48–52
  tailoring of, xiv
Supervisory Working Alliance Inventory, 56
Systematic models, 67–68
Systematic reflection, 72–73
Systematic Treatment Selection (STS), 9, 67–68, 130–131
*Systems of Psychotherapy* (Prochaska), 14

Technical deficits, 107
Technical eclecticism, 9
Technique, preoccupation with, 48
Technique melding, 10
Technology, 135–136
Termination sessions
  acknowledgment of loss during, 119
  emotional reactions in, 76–78
  supervision sessions on, 99–100
Theoretical integration, 9–11
Theory smushing, 10
Therapeutic alliance, 39–40
Therapeutic relationship
  outcome variance and, 8
  promoting and tracking, 39–41
Therapists
  behaviors of supervisors and, 15–16
  as clients, 124
  integrative supervision with expert vs. novice, 32
  personal therapy for, 17, 122–124
  virtual reality in training of, 136
Therapy. *See* Psychotherapy
Thorne, Frederick, 13
Thought experiments, 74
Time limits, for supervision sessions, 101

Timing, for integrative supervision, 31–32
Trainees. *See* Supervisee(s)
Training
  for supervisors, 117–118
  virtual reality in, 136
Transcripts of videotaped sessions, 73
Transdiagnostic patient features
  assessment of, 34–36, 136
  fitting relational behaviors to, 113
  tailoring psychotherapy to, 96
Transtheoretical approach, 10, 14
Treatment adaptation, 90–96
Treatment manuals, 5
Treatment planning, 32–33, 54
Treatment preferences, clients', 38
Treatment selection
  documentation of, 79–80
  legal and ethical issues with, 111–112
  patient features and, 34
  supervisee consternation with, 42
Triple A tie mnemonic, 34
Trust, 51
Tutorials, 79

Uncertainty, 43
Urgencies, clinical, 88

Video recordings, 70–73
Virtual reality, 136
Virtual therapies, 135–136
Vulnerability(-ies)
  clients' and supervisees' expressions of, 98
  of supervisors, 76, 118–119

Wachtel, Paul, 10, 13–14
Wallerstein, R. S., 120
Wampold, Bruce, 7
Worthington, E. L., 56
Written contracts, 45–46, 114

# About the Authors

**John C. Norcross, PhD, ABPP,** is Distinguished Professor of Psychology at the University of Scranton, adjunct professor of psychiatry at State University of New York Upstate Medical University, and a board-certified clinical psychologist. Author of more than 400 scholarly publications, Dr. Norcross has cowritten or edited 25 books, including the five-volume *APA Handbook of Clinical Psychology, Psychotherapy Relationships That Work, Handbook of Psychotherapy Integration, Self-Help That Works, Leaving It at the Office: Psychotherapist Self-Care, Insider's Guide to Graduate Programs in Clinical & Counseling Psychology,* and *Systems of Psychotherapy: A Transtheoretical Analysis,* now in its eighth edition. He was elected the first president of the Society for the Exploration of Psychotherapy Integration and has served as president of the American Psychological Association (APA) Division of Clinical Psychology and the APA Division of Psychotherapy. Dr. Norcross edited the *Journal of Clinical Psychology: In Session* for a decade and has been on the editorial boards of a dozen journals. He has received multiple professional awards, such as APA's Distinguished Career Contributions to Education & Training Award, Pennsylvania Professor of the Year from the Carnegie Foundation, the Rosalee Weiss Award from the American Psychological Foundation, and election to the National Academies of Practice. Dr. Norcross has conducted workshops and lectures in 30 countries. When not traveling, he lives in northeastern Pennsylvania with his wife, two grown children, and two grandkids.

## ABOUT THE AUTHORS

**Leah M. Popple, PsyD,** earned her BA summa cum laude in psychology from Pennsylvania State University and an MA and PsyD in clinical psychology from Marywood University. Her academic awards include Phi Beta Kappa and the Baer-Buell Kappa Alpha Theta Scholarship. Dr. Popple is currently a staff psychologist at the University of Scranton Counseling Center. Her research interests include college student mental health, help-seeking behaviors, and, of course, integrative supervision. Dr. Popple lives in northeastern Pennsylvania with her husband, two daughters, and three tuxedo cats. When not working, she can be found reading, running, cooking, and working in her vegetable garden.

Supervision has clearly come of age as can be witnessed by the profusion of professional guidelines, the proliferation of journals and textbooks, and even the establishment of the American Psychological Association's (APA) Clinical Supervision Essentials series to which this book and its companion DVD, *Integrative Psychotherapy Supervision*, belong. By our recent count, there now exist at least a dozen published guidelines on clinical supervision in the English language around the world. In 2014, APA joined the crowd by offering its own guidance to health service psychologists (https://www.apa.org/about/policy/guidelines-supervision.pdf) and promoting quality supervision across competency domains using evidence-based practices of supervision.

Although supervisor competence is now often defined, it is rarely verified. The educational system continues to assume competent practitioners will make competent supervisors and that bright-enough graduate students will make eager, competent supervisees. Folie à deux!

Supervision represents a complex and demanding activity, and the introduction of an integrative perspective does nothing to relieve the pressure on supervisors and supervisees. On the contrary, the supervision of integrative psychotherapy probably requires more from trainees and their mentors than do single-school therapy systems. Not only must the conventional difficulties in producing competent clinicians be resolved, but an integrative approach must also help supervisees to master treatment combinations and to adjust their therapeutic approach to fit the needs of their clients. Nonetheless, if we are to train psychotherapists more broadly than, in Gardner Murphy's (1969) words, "the subspecialized people we turn out today," an intensive apprenticeship with integrative supervisors is needed.

Integrative psychotherapy supervision thus constitutes at once an exciting challenge and a promising opportunity. In this opening chapter, we outline our theoretical underpinnings, trace the history of psychotherapy integration, and define integrative supervision. Moving from these introductory considerations, we then address our personal paths to integrative supervision.

# Introduction

Students learn psychotherapy primarily through experience and supervision. In large-scale multidisciplinary surveys, clinical supervision is generally rated the second most important contribution to one's professional development, immediately behind direct experience working with patients (e.g., Henry, Sims, & Spray, 1971; Orlinsky & Rønnestad, 2005). Far more than courses and books and theories, hands-on supervision of actual clients constitutes the learning foundation.

Clinical supervision is essential to the education and competence of mental health professionals of all disciplines and orientations. Most mental health professionals will at some point during their career supervise another (Bernard & Goodyear, 2014), and conducting supervision is consistently one of the top five ways in which psychologists spend their professional time (Norcross & Rogan, 2013). More and more, supervision is properly viewed as spanning entire careers of psychologists (Grant & Schofield, 2007).

---

http://dx.doi.org/10.1037/15967-001
*Supervision Essentials for Integrative Psychotherapy*, by J. C. Norcross and L. M. Popple
Copyright © 2017 by the American Psychological Association. All rights reserved.

Supervision Essentials for

# Integrative Psychotherapy

singular and use our initials (JCN, LMP). Otherwise, we speak together throughout the book.

Our use of the term *integrative supervision* deliberatively denotes two meanings: (a) supervision itself that integrates methods, modalities, and mechanisms associated with diverse theoretical orientations; and (b) supervision of psychotherapy conducted from an integrative approach. At times, this ambiguity proves confusing, but we believe it serves the higher purpose of underscoring the inherent parallel processes of integrative supervision. The supervisor remains theoretically flexible in systematically tailoring supervision to the individual trainee, just as that trainee simultaneously adapts psychotherapy to the individual client and singular context. In this respect, the supervision medium becomes much of the message.

So, a warm welcome to our *Supervision Essentials for Integrative Psychotherapy.* The book contains transcripts and analyses of supervisory sessions, including those depicted in the companion DVD, *Integrative Psychotherapy Supervision* (http://www.apa.org/pubs/videos/4310959.aspx), as well as summaries of exciting research on the differential effectiveness of integrative supervision as compared to supervision as usual. We hope it all proves useful and leads you to join us in—or reconfirm your commitment to—integrative supervision, in both desired senses of that term.

- tailoring both the supervision method and the supervisory relationship to the trainee (in contrast to the historical bifurcation of the method and the relationship);
- responsiveness of supervision to multiple supervisory characteristics (instead of a single construct, be that culture, countertransference, or cognitive style); and
- outcome feedback and monitoring of the supervision and, in parallel fashion, of the psychotherapy conducted by the supervisee (as opposed to the supervisor acting as the solitary evaluator of performance).

This book represents a twice-told tale of clinical supervision: once from the perspective of the supervisor and once from the perspective of the supervisee. We find publications from only the supervisor's vantage point seriously incomplete and potentially misleading; it is similar to reading about psychotherapy solely from the practitioner's point of view. Are the intended goals actually accomplished? Is the supervisor's feedback received as intended? Is the supervisor experienced, in fact, as empathic and supportive? Ignoring the other person's experience in any relationship surely constitutes folly, but more so in a deliberately relational and mentoring enterprise as supervision. If we have learned anything from the research on clinical supervision, it is to privilege the supervisee's experience.

Thankfully, APA's Clinical Supervision Essentials DVD series describes supervision from both perspectives. This book follows suit because as therapists and coauthors we inhabit the roles of supervisor (JCN) and supervisee (LMP), respectively. In the DVD, the host of the series inquires about integrative supervision from both the supervisor's and the supervisee's point of view, and although much of this book is written from the perspective of the more experienced supervisor, the unique viewpoint of the supervisee is highlighted throughout as well. This multi-angled collaboration represents an essential part of the learning process, for all parties involved. All supervisors were at one time supervisees themselves, after all, but time and power frequently dull appreciation for the "underling" position.

When speaking from our respective vantage points or about our personal experiences, we switch from the first-person plural to the first-person

# Preface

In the beginning, psychotherapy and its supervision were conducted from a single theoretical orientation and with little regard to outcome research. If eclectic hybrids were offered at all, they were unsystematic and often ineffable conglomerations of personal hunches, common factors, and treasured biases. Those days are gone—for good.

In this volume, we feature systematic and research-informed supervision of integrative psychotherapy. We focus on what is distinctive about integrative supervision: its thoughtful synthesis of supervisory methods and concepts aligned with multiple theoretical traditions; its research-fueled fit of supervision to the individuality of the supervisee; its insistence on frequent feedback from the supervisee about the utility of supervision; and its commitment to modeling the pragmatic flexibility of psychotherapy integration itself.

Of course, many clinical supervisors characterize themselves as integrative; it is, after all, the modal theoretical orientation of mental health professionals (Cook, Biyanova, Elhai, Schnurr, & Coyne, 2010; Norcross & Goldfried, 2005). But in this book we go further than simply acknowledging that clinical reality and supervisee heterogeneity require flexibility. The integrative supervision described and illustrated here rests on

- research evidence for the effectiveness of particular supervisory (and psychotherapy) methods (as opposed to the traditional reliance on theory);

In addition to the books, each expert filmed an actual supervisory session with a supervisee so that her or his approach could be demonstrated in practice. APA Books has produced these videos as a series and they are available as DVDs (http://www.apa.org/pubs/videos). Each of these books and videos can be used together or independently, as part of the series or alone, for the reader aspiring to learn how to supervise, for supervisors wishing to deepen their knowledge, for trainees wanting to be better supervisees, for teachers of courses on supervision, and for researchers investigating this pedagogical process.

## ABOUT THIS BOOK

In this book, *Supervision Essentials for Integrative Psychotherapy*, John C. Norcross and Leah M. Popple describe the background, rationale, and method of supervising psychotherapists in systematic integration. Filled with numerous real-life examples, helpful resources, and evidence-based practice skills, the authors present the integrative supervisory process with a simplicity that is disarming. We trust that you will feel like you are being led through some amazing terrain by expert guides.

We thank you for your interest and hope the books in this series enhance and stimulate your work.

Hanna Levenson and Arpana G. Inman

We see the critical importance of good supervision and its high prevalence. We also have guidelines for its competent practice and an impressive list of objectives. But is this enough to become a good supervisor? Not quite. One of the best ways to learn is from highly regarded supervisors—the experts in the field—those who have the procedural knowledge to know what to do, when, and why.

Which leads us to our motivation for creating this series. As we looked around for materials that would help us supervise, teach, and research clinical supervision, we were struck by the lack of a coordinated effort to present the essential models of supervision in both didactic and experiential forms through the lens of expert supervisors. What seemed to be needed was a forum in which the experts in the field present the basics of their approaches in a readable, accessible, concise fashion and demonstrate what they do in a real supervisory session. The need, in essence, was for a showcase of best practices.

This series, then, is an attempt to do just that. We considered the major approaches to supervisory practice—those based on theoretical orientation and those that are pantheoretical. We surveyed psychologists, educators, clinical supervisors, and researchers throughout the world working in the area of supervision. We asked them to identify specific models to include and who they would consider to be the experts. We also asked this community of colleagues to identify key issues that typically need to be addressed in supervision sessions. Through this consensus building, we came up with a dream team of 11 supervision experts who not only developed a model of supervision but also have worked in the trenches as clinical supervisors for years.

We asked each expert to write a concise book elucidating her or his approach to supervision. This included highlighting the key principles, essential methods/techniques, and structure/process involved, the research evidence for the model, and how common supervisory issues are handled. Furthermore, we asked each author to elucidate the supervisory process by devoting a chapter describing a supervisory session in detail, including transcripts of real sessions, so that the readers could see how the model comes to life in the reality of the supervisory encounter.

# Foreword to the Clinical Supervision Essentials Series

We are both clinical supervisors. We teach courses on supervision of students who are in training to become therapists. We give workshops on supervision and consult with supervisors about their supervision practices. We write and do research on the topic. To say we eat and breathe supervision might be a little exaggerated, but only slightly. We are fully invested in the field and in helping supervisors provide the most informed and helpful guidance to those learning the profession. We also are committed to helping supervisees/trainees become better collaborators in the supervisory endeavor by understanding their responsibilities in the supervisory process.

It is now widely acknowledged in the literature that supervision is a distinct competency in its own right. One cannot assume that being an excellent therapist generalizes to being an outstanding supervisor. Nor can one imagine that good supervisors can just be "instructed" in how to supervise through purely academic, didactic means.

The importance of supervision can be attested to by the increasing numbers of guidelines promulgated by professional associations, of state laws and regulations that certify supervisors, and the required multiple supervisory practica and internships. Furthermore, research has confirmed the high prevalence of supervisory responsibilities among practitioners. Specifically, between 85% and 90% of all therapists eventually become clinical supervisors within their first 15 years of practice.

# Contents

| | |
|---|---|
| Foreword to the Clinical Supervision Essentials Series | vii |
| Preface | xi |
| Chapter 1. Introduction | 3 |
| Chapter 2. Key Principles | 27 |
| Chapter 3. Supervisory Methods | 65 |
| Chapter 4. Structure and Process of Supervision | 87 |
| Chapter 5. Handling Common Supervisory Challenges | 103 |
| Chapter 6. Supervisor Development and Self-Care | 117 |
| Chapter 7. Research Support | 127 |
| Chapter 8. Conclusions and Future Directions | 133 |
| Suggested Readings | 139 |
| References | 141 |
| Index | 159 |
| About the Authors | 167 |

Copyright © 2017 by the American Psychological Association. All rights reserved. Except as permitted under the United States Copyright Act of 1976, no part of this publication may be reproduced or distributed in any form or by any means, including, but not limited to, the process of scanning and digitization, or stored in a database or retrieval system, without the prior written permission of the publisher.

Published by
American Psychological Association
750 First Street, NE
Washington, DC 20002
www.apa.org

To order
APA Order Department
P.O. Box 92984
Washington, DC 20090-2984
Tel: (800) 374-2721; Direct: (202) 336-5510
Fax: (202) 336-5502; TDD/TTY: (202) 336-6123
Online: www.apa.org/pubs/books
E-mail: order@apa.org

In the U.K., Europe, Africa, and the Middle East, copies may be ordered from
American Psychological Association
3 Henrietta Street
Covent Garden, London
WC2E 8LU England

Typeset in Minion by Circle Graphics, Inc., Columbia, MD

Printer: United Book Press, Baltimore, MD
Cover Designer: Mercury Publishing Services, Inc., Rockville, MD

The opinions and statements published are the responsibility of the authors, and such opinions and statements do not necessarily represent the policies of the American Psychological Association.

Library of Congress Cataloging-in-Publication Data

Names: Norcross, John C., 1957- author. | Popple, Leah M., author. | American
   Psychological Association, publisher.
Title: Supervision essentials for integrative psychotherapy / John C. Norcross
   and Leah M. Popple.
Other titles: Clinical supervision essentials series.
Description: First edition. | Washington, DC : American Psychological
   Association, [2017] | Series: Clinical supervision essentials series |
   Includes bibliographical references and index.
Identifiers: LCCN 2016020575| ISBN 9781433826283 | ISBN 1433826283
Subjects: | MESH: Psychotherapy—education | Psychotherapy—methods |
   Clinical Competence
Classification: LCC RC480 | NLM WM 18 | DDC 616.89/14—dc23 LC record available
   at https://lccn.loc.gov/2016020575

British Library Cataloguing-in-Publication Data
A CIP record is available from the British Library.

*Printed in the United States of America*
*First Edition*

http://dx.doi.org/10.1037/15967-000

# CLINICAL SUPERVISION ESSENTIALS

HANNA LEVENSON *and* ARPANA G. INMAN, Series Editors

Supervision Essentials for

# Integrative Psychotherapy

John C. Norcross
and Leah M. Popple

**American Psychological Association • Washington, DC**

# Clinical Supervision Essentials Series

*Supervision Essentials for Psychodynamic Psychotherapies*
 Joan E. Sarnat

*Supervision Essentials for the Integrative Developmental Model*
 Brian W. McNeill and Cal D. Stoltenberg

*Supervision Essentials for the Feminist Psychotherapy Model of Supervision*
 Laura S. Brown

*Supervision Essentials for a Systems Approach to Supervision*
 Elizabeth L. Holloway

*Supervision Essentials for the Critical Events in Psychotherapy Supervision Model*
 Nicholas Ladany, Myrna L. Friedlander, and Mary Lee Nelson

*Supervision Essentials for Existential–Humanistic Therapy*
 Orah T. Krug and Kirk J. Schneider

*Supervision Essentials for Cognitive–Behavioral Therapy*
 Cory F. Newman and Danielle A. Kaplan

*Supervision Essentials for the Practice of Competency-Based Supervision*
 Carol A. Falender and Edward P. Shafranske

*Supervision Essentials for Emotion-Focused Therapy*
 Leslie S. Greenberg and Liliana Ramona Tomescu

*Supervision Essentials for Integrative Psychotherapy*
 John C. Norcross and Leah M. Popple

Supervision Essentials for

# Integrative Psychotherapy

I loved this book. Clearly written, personable, and eminently practical, it is the definitive guide to supervising—and being supervised—from an integrative, eclectic, or pluralistic standpoint. More than that, this unique text details a collaborative, feedback- and evidence-informed approach to supervision that should be essential reading for supervisors of all orientations.

—**Mick Cooper, DPhil, CPsychol,** Professor of Counselling Psychology, University of Roehampton, London, England; and coauthor of *Pluralistic Counselling and Psychotherapy*

This book catapults us into supervision that elegantly fuses evidence-based practice and relational responsiveness. Integrative supervision is the wave of the future, and this engaging text is the GPS to get there. Case illustrations and supervision snippets provide a front row seat to integrative supervision in action.

—**Linda Campbell, PhD,** Professor, University of Georgia, Athens

In these days of learning how to conduct therapy from single-school manuals, it is refreshing to have comprehensive guidelines for how beginning therapists can use an integrative approach to therapy. The guidelines in this volume are based on clinical experience and empirical evidence, and the discussions provide insights into supervision from the vantage points of both supervisor and supervisee.

—**Marvin R. Goldfried, PhD,** past president of the Society for the Exploration of Psychotherapy Integration, and Distinguished Professor of Psychology, Stony Brook University, Stony Brook, NY

This indispensible book is *the* companion on the best and most up-to-date practice in integrative supervision. It is a cutting-edge, compelling read, and an invaluable contribution to the field. It provides a crucial resource for trainees, psychotherapists, supervisees, supervisors, psychologists, and all health care and allied professionals. The evidence-based both/and approach of Norcross and Popple opens up exciting possibilities for supervision as a means of growth not only for the professional but for the profession.

—**Marcella Finnerty, DPsych,** Director of Programmes and Supervisor, Institute of Integrative Counselling and Psychotherapy, Dublin, Ireland